If Kids Could Vote

If Kids Could Vote

Children, Democracy, and the Media

Sally Sugarman

LEXINGTON BOOKS

A division of
ROWMAN & LITTLEFIELD PUBLISHERS, INC.
Lanham • Boulder • New York • Toronto • Plymouth, UK

LEXINGTON BOOKS

A division of Rowman & Littlefield Publishers, Inc.
A wholly owned subsidiary of The Rowman & Littlefield Publishing Group, Inc.
4501 Forbes Boulevard, Suite 200
Lanham, MD 20706

Estover Road
Plymouth PL6 7PY
United Kingdom

British Library Cataloguing in Publication Information Available

Library of Congress Cataloging-in-Publication Data

Sugarman, Sally.
 If kids could vote : children, democracy, and the media / Sally Sugarman.
    p. cm.
 Includes bibliographical references and index.
 ISBN-13: 978-0-7391-1395-0 (cloth : alk. paper)
 ISBN-10: 0-7391-1395-X (cloth : alk. paper)
 ISBN-13: 978-0-7391-1396-7 (pbk. : alk. paper)
 ISBN-10: 0-7391-1396-8 (pbk. : alk. paper)
 1. Children and politics. 2. Mass media and children—United States. 3. Political
socialization—United States. 4. Democracy—United States. 5. Elections—United
States. 6. Children—United States--Attitudes. I. Title.
 HQ784.P5S84 2007
 306.20973—dc22   2006030165

Printed in the United States of America

♾™ The paper used in this publication meets the minimum requirements of American
National Standard for Information Sciences—Permanence of Paper for Printed Library
Materials, ANSI/NISO Z39.48–1992.

For my family
and all the thoughtful children I interviewed and surveyed.

Contents

Acknowledgments

This book would not have happened without the cooperation of many people. The Southwest Supervisory Union of Vermont was most generous in allowing its students and teachers to be surveyed over a number of years. Those students, principals, and teachers are gratefully acknowledged. Shaftsbury School generously loaned me the fifth and sixth grade textbooks. Special thanks must go to Jerry O'Connor and Nancy Bohne whose classes over the years were the sites where I did my interviews. Thanks also to Pamela DeFelice, Kevin Donahue and Cynthia Kilgallon who distributed surveys to expand the population that I studied.

My greatest debt is to the students and teachers who were surveyed and the young people whom I interviewed. However, the book could not have been written without the support of my husband Bob, who both by his example and his willingness to take on extra tasks, made it possible for me to complete this work.

Chapter One

The Changing Nature of Childhood and the Media

Examining children's ideas about democracy has significance on many levels. Children reflect what a society thinks is important for its citizenry to believe. In school, children are specifically taught about the government and democracy. However, children are not merely mirrors that provide images of what the society tells them. They actively construct their own ideas from information and attitudes they glean from the adults around them, both those they know personally and those they know from the media. This does not mean that they are necessarily predictors of what the next generation will think and do when it achieves the status of voter. The situation is more complex than that. Children do provide a perspective on what the society values, but perceived through the prism of dependency. The powerless are by their very position astute observers of the powerful. They may not be accurate observers, but they are sensitive to the underlying themes in the messages that the society offers them. Whether their views change over time and whether that change is the result of biological maturity or a change in social status or both requires a more extended study than the present one.

This study will look at some specific children as they ponder the questions of democracy and citizenship. It will also examine some of the media that engages them. What do children learn about democracy from Harry Potter and Sponge Bob? Listening to adults, some of them believe that the media teach children a great deal, and not all of the lessons are beneficial.

The images that children see in films and on television create an atmosphere in which children develop their ideas about power and danger. When 9/11 occurred, children were confronted with images with which they were familiar from disaster movies. Similarly, children saw the aftermath of hurricane Katrina on their television screens. Although images provide a sense of the reality and immediacy of the event, it is still language that supplies the necessary narrative and politicians and news commentators quickly supplied an interpretation of the events. Although there was no doubt that the horror of these moments had their own reality, the events became incorporated into the mythic tale of democracy always under attack. Endangered democracy is the unifying theme that rallies a diverse population at moments of crisis. This is echoed in the country's national anthem with "bombs bursting in air."

In many ways, contemporary media empowers children. There are many Internet sites that inform them while allowing an interaction that may be quite different from that of their classrooms. Some of these sites deal with politics; others are reflections of popular culture, selling or entertaining. Even television programs whose format invites more passivity than the Internet or video games often ask children to participate in different ways, by voting for some of their favorite performers or sending in answers to riddles.

Children's political socialization has been studied from a number of different perspectives, sometimes indirectly as in the examination of texts and novels and picture books as well as the visual media. Sometimes more directly. Research in the 1960s and 1970s recognized the impact of popular entertainment in providing a range of role models for children that were different from those of children living in a primarily print culture.[1] Television, particularly as it depicted the Vietnamese war, influenced children and adults alike. At that time children surveyed saw the President as the most powerful person in the country. They generally had respect for both the office and the individual. In 2002, a study replicating some of the early research showed that while children still respected the office, they were more critical of the individuals who held it.[2]

During the 1972 election, Thomas Cottle[3] interviewed two black children, a boy and a girl, aged twelve, from the Roxbury section of Boston. Depending on their life experiences, children have different perceptions of the information that the society provides them. Cottle wanted to explore that idea with these extended interviews, making no claims that he was describing more than these children and their families. The boy, after explaining to Cottle that elections were fixed, and answering Cottle's question about why people would vote, said.

> They vote. . . because they want to think they have something to say in what's going on in the country. They're not even that bothered if they don't; they just want to *believe* that someone up there's listening to 'em and watching the way they vote and think. That's why. No one likes to feel he ain't part of something that's going on. So they vote. That's why *you* vote, probably, isn't it? You don't like being left out.[4]

Voices of children from the "other America" have been muted since Michael Harrington[5] first introduced the concept. Although we know that 20 percent of children live in poverty, it does not seem to register in the same way that it did in the 1960s and 1970s. These children, however, feel the effect of politics differently than do middle-class children. Jonathan Kozol[6] documents some of these impacts in the books that he has written about urban education. It is in the newly segregated schools that children often experience politics in action. No Child Left Behind is supposed to help these children, but underfunding is a powerful political tool.

Besides viewing politics differently, Nightingale[7] claims that poor, black, urban children also experience the media differently than do other children, not only because of the number of times they watch violent movies, but because the violence on the screen connects with the violence on their streets. As Cottle found that black children rejected the images of white politicians as having no significance for them in their lives, so the images they see of themselves on television may be confusing. Although there have been more diverse images offered from Sesame Street on, it is still tinged with negativity.

David Buckingham[8] specifically examined the impact of television on children's political ideas. In his 1996-1997 study he had groups of students, ages twelve to seventeen, look at and discuss Channel One and Nick News in the United States and First Edition and Wise Up in the United Kingdom. These programs are aimed at young people. His groups were of mixed gender. He also had low income and black students among his informants.

When confronted with media clips of different news stories from selected programs, students focussed on the composition of the shots and the backgrounds, rather than listening to the point that the film was trying to make. The older students were more adept at this, demonstrating that years of watching television had made them critical viewers of visual techniques, but not of the substance of the news story itself.

Although adults have been concerned for years about popular culture and children's moral development, this worry intensified in the twentieth and twenty-first centuries. The pleasurable has always been suspect. Chap books, fairy tales, penny dreadfuls, dime novels, comic books, radio, film, television, video games and the Internet; the dangers to children seem to multiply. As Plato famously asked, "Then shall we simply allow our children to listen to any stories that anyone happens to make up, and so receive into their minds ideas often the very opposite of those we shall think they ought to have when they are grown up?"[9]

In a provocative and prescient article written more than thirty years ago, the economist Robert Heilbroner[10] proposed that political ideas are shaped in the crucible of infancy with the reality of children's helplessness. Although children may first feel omnipotent, they quickly recognize their dependency. Heilbroner sees in this a tendency towards submission to a leader who will protect and reassure the individual. Of course, as Erikson[11] noted, ambivalence is born in infancy when the source of pleasure becomes a source of pain during the teething process. Throughout life, individuals vacillate, as they did in childhood, between assertion and dependence. Children may want to emulate or may admire the celebrity and power of the political or media figure, representing the first parent, but they also often chafe under that parent's power. However, Heilbroner's observation that the role of the citizen is to some degree shaped by the lessons learned in the crib and the sandbox has validity.

Klaus Riegel[12] posited the developing child in the changing world and it is this formulation that has guided many of the studies of children's ideas about politics. The idea that there is a developmental progression of thinking comes from Piaget's[13] work. However, children like adults not only formulate their ideas according to their age, but also according to their status in the world. If a child is female, poor and of color living in an urban area, her view of the world differs from that of a white, wealthy male born in a rural Southern home. Robert Coles in his extensive studies of children[14] not only shows this, but also demonstrates how these class positions are continuously reinforced by experiences in everyday life. In *Privileged Ones*,[15] Coles records how the schools and the home work together to reinforce wealthy children's acceptance of the status quo.

Children in the United States from the beginning of the nation's history were children of the modern age if we define modernism as including change as one of its characteristics. Other than native Americans, the families of the children who came to the Untied States were all immigrants. Even those born in the colonies experienced a world far different from that of their parents' childhood. As the country expanded, the topography of childhood was constantly changing. Margaret Mead[16] pointed out that this continued into the technological age where children were still experiencing a different world from that of their parents.

Under these conditions, simple indoctrination of children is difficult. Schools were the vehicle by which adults tried to pass on their ideas to their children or to other people's children in the case of new waves of immigration. Democracy, or at least the idea of democracy, was one of the unifying ideas that was supposed to shape the political fabric of the nation. The public school was to be the fulcrum upon which children built their ideas of democracy. However, from the early days of the republic, children's education was separated according to status and wealth. Schools were never as democratic in their economic demographics as the myth of the one-room school liked to suggest. Schools were also challenged by popular culture. Although not as extensive as it would become in the radio and television age, the secular, commercial world provided children with alternate perspectives through cheap literature, circuses, vaudeville, amusement parks and the expanding toy industry. Nasaw[17] recounts how urban working children at the turn of the nineteenth century kept some of their earnings to pay for the pleasures of the nickelodeon and street corner games. To counter-balance these attractions, Progressive reformers created parks, zoos and more benign amusements for children.

Then as now, school had to compete with these other distractions. Still for all children, the function of schools was one of control. Recognizing this, John Dewey wanted to create a different type of school experience for children. In many ways he wanted to demonstrate democracy by giving children an opportunity to be active learners. However, his ideas were and still are constantly under attack because many adults see his recommendations as spoiling children by challenging the adult's authority over children. Many of the ills of contemporary education are laid at Dewey's[18] door as if his philosophy had been more extensively practiced than it was. Yet democracy as an ideal was manifest in the idea that all children should be provided with publicly supported schools. Although after the Civil War African American children were given sub-standard schools, in theory at least, they were educated in contrast to the prohibition on learning during slavery.

What is most significant about popular culture in the contemporary world is its scope. When John F. Kennedy was assassinated, children throughout the United States were able to see events along with their parents. As indicated earlier, not only did television provide an opportunity for the rituals of mourning to be shared, but children also watched the assassination of his assassin played and replayed on television. No longer were middle class children protected from the realities of death. In their studies of children's reactions, the researchers in Wolfenstein and Kliman's[19] book, noted that children and adults responded differently and that children had shorter sadness spans, causing misunderstandings between the adults and the children. There were also differences in the children's responses based on gender. Psychoanalytical in their analysis, the authors place a great deal of emphasis on the developmental aspects of the assassination of a father figure. This crisis brought politics into the lives of children in a way that interacted with their own developmental stage and personal history.

Five years later, succeeding groups of children saw multiple assassinations when Martin Luther King, Jr., and Robert Kennedy were killed. With 24/7 news broadcasts, children are now constantly confronted with events and commentary on events, not directed at them but having an impact on them. The media recognized this during the first Gulf War when Peter Jennings had a program with children talking about the war.

Postman and Meyrowitz[20] examine how the media affect social discourse about politics. Postman saw the media trivializing politics. On the other hand, Meyrowitz saw the media undermining faith in the country's leaders and in the political system as children and adults saw behind the scenes of not only politics, but all professional agencies. Hospitals, police stations and other venues lost their mystery as viewers observed the dynamics behind the actions of those in responsible positions. Meyrowitz also noted that people stare at people on television, as they never would in face-to-face encounters. While film made leaders larger than life, the television screen diminished them.

Democracy was an ideal based on the notion of the rational discourse of well-informed men who would make decisions after reviewing the information available about the candidates. The reality, of course, was never as pristine as this formulation suggests. Competing interests were always in play. Rationality is always more ideal than actual. However, even this eighteenth century notion of democracy is challenged by the realities of contemporary politics. The expansion of the franchise over the centuries has not noticeably led to more coherence in politics. An expanded electorate is not necessarily better informed. The media, because of their nature which is to show conflict in an entertaining light, reinforce some of the misconceptions of what it means to be a citizen. Joel Spring[21] maintains that democracy has been reduced to having the freedom to make educated choices about what you should buy. We sell our Presidents like other consumer items, an idea first elaborated in *The Selling of the President 1968.*[22]

Spring warns us that the function of a program like Channel One is to provide commercial access to children. The Channel is the enormously successful business that it is because, although provided free to students, the company charges the commercial sponsors heavily for their opportunity to broadcast to a captive audience. In a study about students' reactions to Channel One, *Harvesting Minds*,[23] the researcher found that what the students remembered were the commercials and that their complaint against the station was that they didn't change the commercials frequently enough.

Discussing democracy, a number of writers[24] point out that voting once every four years or even more frequently in local and state as well as federal elections does not provide the voter power equal to that of those with large economic and social resources. Recently, much has been made of the notion of social capital. The social resources individuals have available to them through networks of family, friend and community organizations have an impact on their lives. The nature of children's social capital seems embedded in the status of their parents, the health of their neighborhoods and the quality of their schools.

Even the idea of childhood, shifting according to national and class boundaries, does not belong exclusively to children. Childhood may not be a question of age, but of economic and social position. Those without resources are often treated as if they were children. During the years of segregation, an adult African American male was often referred to as "boy." The humorist Art Buchwald once asked how one would feel if he were half the size of everyone else with no money in his pocket. With girls, unless they were wearing jeans, they might not even have pockets.

Currently the discourse about democracy focuses on voting as if voting were the sole criteria of its efficacy. We must remember however that democracy has a history of excluding people from the electoral process. In colonial United States, for example, those who voted were landed, white men who considered themselves inheritors of the Enlightenment. John Adams brushed aside his wife's request to "Remember the ladies" and black males were not even considered fully human. Their three-fifths status gave additional political power to their white owners, but did not benefit blacks in any way.

So what is democracy? George Kelly,[25] the personal construct theorist, said if you want to know something about people, ask them. However, who is asked and who answers this question is in itself a mark of status and power. Children who are asked this question are not usually expected to come up with their own answers, but to repeat the particular formulation of their particular schooling. There is also a difference between reporting what people say and understanding what they are telling you. What is the context in which children are questioned? Researchers into the lives of children are constantly dealing with the problem of a power differential. Are children telling adults what they think or what they think adults want to hear. Subjects of inquiry have their own power, the power of the weak. The nature of people's power shapes individuals as surely as any aspect of their lives. The argument might then be made that infancy is true democracy since all are equally helpless. However, is this true? Is the child born to a poor mother the same as the child born to a rich father? Is a child born in a poor country the same as one born in a rich country? Is the child, born with a disability the same as a child born healthy? Is the child born female the same as a child born male? Even within the kingdom of infancy, distinctions are evident both in the child's potential and actual circumstances. What does this mean for the development of democracy? How does one educate children to become citizens of a democracy?

These are simple questions, but simple questions usually have complex answers. Part of education is to question that which is simple. What do we mean by play, by family, by childhood? If we ask children these questions, will their answers differ from those that adults will give? Will they differ if it is a female teacher asking them in their classrooms or a male psychologist, having taken the children from that classroom? Will they raise these questions among themselves or do they have other ways of talking about these issues? Will we learn what they think by listening to their stories or by looking at what they think of the stories we tell them?

There are many ways in which we tell children stories. We tell stories about the country's history in schoolbooks, in songs, and in holiday rituals. In contemporary life, besides oral and written tales, we have the stories of the media in film, television and video games. We have always told children stories through the games we provide them, through the toys we offer them. Segments of our society devote themselves to worrying about those stories. Censorship can be justified in the name of protecting the children. Adults may abuse children in many ways, beating them, exploiting them, starving them, but it is the power of stories that will engage adults as few other causes will. Some have suggested that this is easier than dealing with the actual problems and needs of children.[26] A comic book, a video game, a television program has untold influence over children or so some guardians of childhood claim. Just as fairy tales corrupted youth in earlier times so will these media manifestations undermine the foundations of children's well being. What draws children to these unhealthy tales that even Plato warned about? Is it the images of power in He-Man, Ninja Turtles, Pokemon or the latest animated hero that provide children with the compensation that they crave? Do Barbie, the Olsen Twins or The Bratz dolls promise girls that in sex they can find an equalizer for themselves? Is it the conflict in gory stories that has captured the imagination of generations of children or is it the predictability of the messages that reassures children? No matter what horrors occur, the stories will have a satisfactory ending. These endings do not necessarily have to be happy because we do have the tragic story to remind us of death. However, these deaths will be noble and worthy. Lear will regain his honor and his daughter and be mourned. Young men will die in battle for democracy and freedom or for Islam or some other noble cause. Death will come, but it will not be mean or meaningless.

Do the stories help us understand the world or to endure it? The joke goes that the optimist thinks this is the best of all possible worlds and the pessimist

knows it. Stories, however, are specific to their times. There are stories that societies need to deal with their particular circumstances. Are the stories for children and adults different? Or are they only perceived differently? Many would
claim that it is necessary to tell children modified stories appropriate to their age
and understanding. This then becomes woven into a highly detailed and intricate
story for adults about how children develop over time.

Are stories for children and adults different in a technological age than they
were in a preliterate age? Television, like the storyteller around the campfire,
addresses the same audience. If we have a story about democracy, how do children who spend a great deal of time in authoritarian situations like schools hear
that story? Buckingham[27] makes the point that the so-called apathy of young
people may be due to their powerlessness to affect what happens because of
their lack of the vote. He also claims that whatever lessons about democracy are
taught, the message is undercut by the undemocratic nature of schools. Students
experiencing an institution in which they have limited say, see authoritarianism,
not democracy, in action

Is it different for children than it is for the unemployed factory worker? In
the United States in the twenty-first century, race, class and gender are still
meaningful categories in terms of power and politics. Recognizing the limita-
tions of our research, we will look at how some specific children feel about the
stories that the media, schools and parents tell them about the nature of democracy. Living in the Northeastern United States, their responses may be different
than those of children in other parts of the country. However, they are consumers of the same media tales as children throughout the country. We will try to
test how these shared lessons reflect and shape the political system in which
citizens in the United States live.

To what degree does any one group tell us about other groups and larger
groups of individuals? Particular respondents lead us to the questions that we
need to ask on a larger scale. They may be indicators for directions in which
research should move. They will assuredly capture moments in time and place.
It is not only the specific data that we collect, but also the interpretation of that
data that will lead us to some understanding of the process by which young children become citizens of a particular nation at a particular moment in history.

Politics is about many things. However, essentially politics is about power
as Machiavelli pointed out many centuries ago. Power is a force children understand even before they are able to articulate ideas about it. A four-year-old child
may note that "God is the boss of the world" as he struggles to coordinate theol-
ogy into the reality of his life. However, politics also requires knowledge of how
a government as well as how a society works. Besides knowledge, there are attitudes. How do people feel about what they know? How deep is the knowledge
and how consistent are the feelings? What changes one's views about politics?

Politicians place a great deal of emphasis on the stories they tell the public.
They are as fetishistic about naming objects as any child or preliterate. Domestic
spying or terrorist surveillance; social security or personal investment accounts
encapsulate complex narratives. These are narratives that may be presented directly as in speeches, social studies lessons or historical texts. They may also be

conveyed indirectly through fictional tales, such as comic books, movies, television series and video games. During World War II, for example, superheroes fought the Nazis and the "Japs." With Superman on America's side, children may have wondered why winning the war took so long. Perhaps the fact that the villains reappeared or new ones took their places in each month's new comic book helped children understand, as child television viewers of He Man would, that fighting the forces of evil is endless.

Are the tales told children different in content from those told adults or only in form? After Hiroshima, after the war, the "Japs" became the Japanese and role models for our schools and our economy. In what ways do adults have a firmer sense of the real and the make-believe than do children. Recently, the Republicans have been quoted[28] as saying that they create their own reality. To some degree, everyone does. The question is how accurately an individual's construction of reality matches external circumstances. The more power one has the more one theoretically should be able to shape those circumstances to one's ideas. That would seem to be the basis of the Republicans' claim. Those with power can bend the world to their will. Powerful individuals and nations seem to have shared this belief.

If, as Heilbroner[29] claims, the first lesson that the powerless infant learns is obedience, what changes some of those dependent infants into powerful adults. Is it temperament, circumstances or a combination of these and other factors? One of the ongoing conundrums of childhood is this process of transforming from child to adult. In the Bible St Paul says, "When I was a child, I spake as a child, I understood as a child, I thought as a child; but when I became a man I put away childish things."[30] How this occurs has been analyzed continuously. The debates about this issue arise from different constructs about the nature of human development. There are behaviorists who see people as conditioned by pleasure and pain. Much of the basis of our capitalist economy is based on the idea, shared by Freudians and behaviorists, that there is a core of irrationality that fuels people's behavior. Questioning this mechanistic view are the constructivists who see people as both more active and more rational. According to this view, even children are developing and revising their ideas about the world and people. Even within the crib, children are not totally powerless.

Democracy theoretically challenges the configuration of the ruler and the ruled. The revolutions of the oppressed have traditionally been seen as changing the culture of society, if not the underlying power structures. Pinel released the insane from their bondage in the Bastille, the American Civil War freed the slaves and the October Revolution honored the workers. Countering these movements have been dictatorships of all types. Alice Miller[31] contends that, at least in terms of the German example, the excesses of Hitler were traceable to the authoritarian child rearing methods of the German people. Many in the United States feel that the crucible of democracy rests in a more equitable and non-authoritarian child rearing philosophy if not practice. Others are concerned that children in the United States are given too much power.

In *Civilization and Its Discontents*[32] Freud pointed out that there are three factors with which humans have to contend and over which they have limited, if any control; nature, other people and their own divided selves. At its best, the world is somewhat paradoxical. The more power one has to shape the world to one's fancies, the further one gets from the realities of other people's existences, thereby losing information that might be useful. Although we need to gather evidence, how we understand that evidence is crucial, as is the ability to convince others that our interpretation of the evidence is viable.

Often overlooked in politics is a basic rule of scholarship, which is that we have to look at evidence that contradicts our construction of the world. To fully understand religion, we must listen to the arguments of atheists. We must be able to account for evidence that challenges our conclusions. How does this work when we are trying to gauge the knowledge and understanding children bring to politics? We must try, not only for a varied population, but also explore other ways in which the information could be understood.

Although a great deal can be learned by examining wide contrasts such as third world children with those in first world countries, this study will limit itself to a small group of children in the United States. We must note, however, how language affects our constructs; just the use of first and third world has implications of superiority and inferiority. Any study has to be clear what it does not include as well as what it does.

Much work has assumed that changes in children's perspectives on power are the result of changes in cognitive and social development. The idea of stages of development at the heart of the study of childhood has been challenged recently by the advent of contemporary media that provide children access to knowledge that for some children had been unavailable. Although children are isolated from many aspects of the adult world through the medium of schools, changes in the family have eroded one layer of insulation that protected middle class children from some of society's realities.

Anthropologists, from Margaret Mead onward have shown how the material circumstances of a child's world shape development in ways hardly conscious to the individual. Whether the child sleeps on a dirt floor in an Indian village home or in a separate room in a Canadian household influences the reality and the identity of the growing person. The Mickey Mouse T-shirt worn by a child in a Peruvian tribal society reflects a different experience than the same T-shirt worn by a child in suburban Connecticut. The global village and economy are more complex in the lives of children than any reductive analysis suggests. Framing our questions to explore these complexities means crossing disciplinary boundaries as we try to locate particular children at particular times and consider the paths of their development into adults in particular societies.

Historians have also made the point that children at different ages experience the events of their times differently. This has led to an examination of different cohorts. In his study on the Great Depression, Elder[33] made it clear that this economic and social event had a different impact on children, depending on their age and gender. It is this complexity that must be kept in mind as we study children's ideas about democracy and the ways in which the media influence them. Form and content must also be analyzed separately and in conjunction with each other. The way in which a message is told is significant in terms of the amount of involvement the child has in it. A popular slogan of the educational reform movement of the 1970s was, I hear and I forget, I see and I remember, I do and I understand.

Examining the media has often been done through an analysis of texts, but as important as that is, it is also necessary to investigate how children at different ages and in different circumstances interpret those texts. We can extract the messages that are being sent, but we also have to know how those messages are being received. One assumption that needs to be tested is that individuals will decode these messages differently based on age, race, gender and class. Although statistical evidence suggests that there are more differences within groups than between groups, it will be informative to find out if there are any consistent group perspectives that emerge. What is the nature of those whose views are different from those of the group? What is the relationship between what people say and what they do? How do people interpret their own actions as contrasted with the actions of others? In some conversations with children, it is interesting that none of them believe in censorship for themselves, but do think that those younger than themselves should be protected. What is the source of this view? Is it altruistic or does it suggest that one finds superiority wherever one can?

First, we must assess children's knowledge, not only of government, but also of society. Then we need to look at attitudes and then behavior. How do children explain their own actions and that of others? What impact do various media have on these three elements? The media to be examined will be children's books, television programs, commercials, Internet sites and video games. Textual analysis will be supplemented with group interviews of children, surveys and interviews with adults.

Change is characteristic of contemporary society. Change has been a part of the history of the United States, even more than of other nations, given its status as a nation of immigrants. Children have changed according to the circumstances of their lives even though many have tried to fix childhood in an unchanging pattern of development that would transcend particulars of place and time. Erik Erikson's[34] powerful evocation of the stages of childhood emerges from the circumstances of the 1950s. It was a lens through which many viewed not only children of that time but of other historical periods. However, for females particularly, the theory's origin in a specific historical period became evident as the circumstances of their lives changed. Educating females has had unintended consequences as the history of the feminist movement demonstrates.

Even biological growth that would seem to have some predictable patterns is affected by factors such as nutrition, environment and social expectations. Accounts of children on the western frontier remind us that the idea of children growing up quickly is not just a result of exposure to the media as Postman[35] contends. Although childhood lost in factories was decried, the more isolated and free ranging life of farm children was not as noted as was their presence in the gold and silver mining camps where adult influence was thought to be detrimental to children's growth, physically and morally. Yet these children, according to the data historian Elliot West[36] provides, grew up no more or less immoral than children in other circumstances.

What are the consequences of relinquishing the idea of a universal childhood in which individuals emerge into a society in a logical sequence of cognitive, emotional and social growth? The idea of children's rights emerged from many of the political conflicts of the 1960s and 1970s. The nature of children's sexuality was one of the thorniest issues that the children's rights agenda confronted. Just as Freud's theories of infantile sexuality bewildered and outraged many, making the distinction between sexual abuse and sexual freedom for children was debated. How much should children be controlled and how much should adults? Parents photographing their children in the nude came under suspicion, as did overly friendly neighbors. These are not simple issues and they are rarely addressed without much emotion on all sides. The international declaration of the rights of children, to which the United States has not subscribed, attempts to offer some clarification.

There is a difference between the construct of childhood as a set of principles guiding adult responsibility and behavior towards children and the experience of childhood by particular children of various ages living in distinct times and places. What are the rights of the non-verbal, relatively immobile six months old and the articulate and active eleven-year-old? Some may consider this an extension of the debate about the rights of the fetus. The inconsistency in people's views about this continuum is a political matter in which children of all ages have relatively little power to affect the discourse much less the actions of the adults.

This is complicated by the role of childhood in the life span. In societies in which many children died before the age of five and normal adults lived into their forties, childhood had a different meaning and emotional affect. It is an over-simplification to say that adulthood began at puberty, but in many ways it did. However, when the adult life span has been extended into the seventies, the relationship between childhood and adulthood changed dramatically. Many[37] have noted the competition between children and seniors for society's resources. Individuals are also more distanced from their own childhood, although as Lee[38] has pointed out, the definition of adulthood as a stable time of life has also changed. The distinction between children and adults in terms of becoming and being has weakened.

Contemporary constructs of childhood are as much a product of their time as were earlier constructs. This does not mean that they are not useful. Indeed we can note some of the changes in children's experiences by looking at the theories that evolve to explain them. As new theories of childhood emerge, they reflect changes in the material circumstances of children's lives in the United States. Some of these changes are evident in other parts of the world as well. However, as we focus on the United States, we can detect differences based on race, class and gender.

The ratio of children's direct to indirect experience has changed dramatically. Not only do urban children have less direct knowledge of the natural world, they also have less contact with a variety of individuals compared to the range of people they can see in film, television and video games. This is true even in rural areas of the country where the technology pervades the home and the school. The world has become more abstract for children as they work at computers and watch television and VCRs. Baudrillard suggests that the image of reality is so powerful that it is difficult to tell it from reality.[39] From infancy on some children are encouraged to see shapes and colors and hear music and language through supposedly cognitive enhancing materials such as Infant Shakespeare videotapes, rather than listen to a human voice or hold a red cube.

The structure of the family has also changed. Not only is there less contact with family members who may live many miles away, available only through instant messaging or cell phone contact, but more families are blended families. Or as a college student described it, they are accordion families, where divorces and remarriage may lead to a variety of siblings who come and go as the parental figures change. Half of all marriages end in divorce, resulting in a large number of children who spend at least part of their lives before the age of eighteen in a single parent household or migrating between two families. Even in two parent families, both parents may be working, shifting some responsibilities on to the children as rural families once did.

As a result of the increased working hours of both parents, children become members of peer groups at earlier and earlier ages for longer periods of time. In the past, peer group relationships were seen as important in the middle years of childhood. Now preschool aged children have complex group relationships both inside and outside of school.

An argument can be made that the family has always been changing and in modern societies this is true. Histories of the family provide convincing evidence of that. Within larger social trends there are also specific group differences. The experiences of immigrant children, of children fleeing from war zones, of children of poverty and of wealth are unique although many of the larger social circumstances affect them all even if in different ways. Wars, depressions, natural disasters, technological change are factors that touch the lives of all children. Bronfenbrenner[40] postulated a theory that looks at childhood on a variety of levels from the direct to the indirect, from dyadic relationships to influences from the larger social forces that impinge indirectly, but no less powerfully, on the individual.

Along with, and a part of, this social milieu has been the impact of the media. Besides print, which requires a certain amount of skill to interpret, radio, television and computers have made information more accessible to children at earlier and earlier ages. Although children may be isolated from most adults by their confinement in schools, they have access to images of adults through the media. These images are not the same as actual adults who are complex beings. The images are simplified, glorified and they do not respond to their audience. The images may reflect some ideas of the audience but they are relatively immutable. The rise of fan fiction may be a response to a desire to be able to affect these images and have them conform to the audience's views. Play is another way in which children exert some control. A Barbie in the hands of a seven-year-old girl, much less a seven-year-old boy, is not only the object that Mattel created as many accounts and research indicates,[41] but is also an instrument of the child's conflicting emotions about sex and power.

In the United States, more than in other nations, the media have been a commercial enterprise. Although recently the government has been using the media more as other countries have as a political tool, essentially the media have been in the business of selling products. Not only are children constantly exposed to branded environments, but also because distrust has grown up about this commercial aspect of the media, children have been enlisted to help the media sell its products. Ironically, this leads to further disempowerment of children since the children's ideas become the intellectual property of the companies that have encouraged the children's participation.

The media have changed not only in the content, but also in form. These forms may be as significant as any messages that they convey. Just as print was thought to produce a certain type of sequential, logical thinking that initially produced the idea of democracy, so the visual media are claimed to be changing the nature of children's minds.[42] Video games are particularly potent because they provide an opportunity for interaction within a framework, differently from that of television where the only action available is to change the channels. Computer children are thought to be like the immigrant children of the nineteenth and early twentieth century, knowing more than their parents do about the new culture. Mead[43] made this claim for television and it is even more true of the video game and Internet generation. Although we may not want to romanticize the children as millennials, as much as Howe and Strauss[44] do, the technology does empower them as well as giving them new vehicles for constructing their ideas about the world in which they live. We will investigate some of the ways in which the children not only get messages from the media, but also use the media to construct their own worlds.

Although children as young as five can articulate their ideas about power and issues of moral values such as the nature of fairness and good and bad, they are still relatively inexperienced and in a vulnerable position different from that of older children who have more independence. Children provide strange echoes of adult discourse. When a seven-year-old girl looking at an assortment of colorful pool toys can pick up a blue plastic hand grenade and wonder aloud, "What messages are they sending children?" we do not necessarily gain insight into the thought processes of this age group, but awareness of the ubiquity of these type of facile questions. Yet this should not lead us to underestimate the thinking of children when seriously engaged in discussing matters of immediate concern to them. Matthews[45] has shown that children can be engaged in serious philosophical discussions if time is taken to listen and question them respectfully.

Children in the sixth grade of elementary schools are articulate and not yet troubled by some of the issues that they will face in adolescence. Sexuality is not absent from their lives, but it is not the preoccupation that it will be in the immediate future. More independent of adults, but still children, this group offers an interesting view into the developing ideas about the world of politics. As an age group, they are generally perceived in traditional developmental psychology to have achieved a cognitive maturity that can deal with abstract thought. In most school systems, they are at the top of the elementary school ladder and have some confidence in their mastery of some subject, either in school or out of school. They are at the crossroads of childhood and adolescence. This is also the point at which Gilligan[46] and other researchers see a major readjustment in the female's idea of herself.

Presidential elections focus the attention of the nation on the issue of democracy. Elongated political campaigns saturate the airwaves with claims and counter claims about how the nation should be governed. Television, the Internet and the classroom declare to children that this is an important moment when democracy is demonstrated in action. In this study children were interviewed and surveyed during three presidential election and one non-presidential election years. This study began when the nation was at peace. It was concluded when the nation was at war. Even though the children interviewed and surveyed are different at each time period, the impact of major events on children's thinking is evident. As during the civil rights movement and the Vietnam War, the impact of the media on children's ideas is intensified at such moments. During World War II children were exposed to patriotic war movies, the radio and weekly filmed news reports in the theatres. Posters, newspapers, magazines and other print media also assailed them. However, with the advent of 24/7 news programs as well as the Internet with its invitation to respond to the news, children experience an intensity of messages that may be unique in the history of childhood.

How do these messages prepare them to be citizens of a democracy? Through interviews, surveys and analysis of texts, this study will attempt to address that question.

Notes

1. R.W.Connell, *The Child's Construction of Politics* (Carlton, Victoria: Melbourne University Press, 1971), Fred I. Greenstein,. *Children and Politics* (New Haven: Yale University Press, 1965) and Robert D. Hess and Judith V. Torney. *The Development of Political Attitudes in Children.* (Garden City, New York: Doubleday and Co., 1967).

2. Amy Carter and Ryan L Teten. "Assessing Changing Views of the President: Revisiting Greenstein's Children and Politics" *Presidential Studies Quarterly,* 32, no.3 (*Sept* 2002) 453(10).

3. Thomas Cottle, *Black Children, White Dreams* (New York: Delta Pub. Co., 1974).

4. Cottle, *Black Children,* 32.

5. Michael Harrington, *The Other America* (New York: The Macmillan Company, 1963).

6. Jonathan Kozol, *Ordinary Resurrections.* (New York: Crown Publishers, 2000), *Amazing Grace* (New York: Crown Publishers, 1995) and *Savage Inequalities* (New York: Crown Publishers, 1991).

7. Carl H. Nightingale, *On the Edge* (New York: Basic Books, 1993).

8. David Buckingham, *The Making of Citizens: Young People, News and Politics* (London: Routlege, 2003).

9. Francis Macdonald Cornford, *The Republic of Plato* (New York: Oxford University Press, 1965), 69.

10. Robert L. Heilbroner, "The Human Prospect" *The New York Review of Books,* 20, no 21 and 22 (Jan 24, 1974) 21-34.

11. Erik Erikson, *Childhood and Society* (New York: W.W. Norton and Company, Inc. 1990).

12. Klaus F. Riegel, "Toward a Dialectical Theory of Development," in *The Development of Dialectical Operations,* ed Klaus F. Rigel (Basel, Switzerland: S. Karger, 1975), 50-64.

13. Jean Piaget, *The Language and Thought of the Child* (New York: Meridan Books, 1960),

14. Robert Coles, *The Political Life of Children* (Boston: Houghton Mifflin Co., 1986).

15. Robert Coles, *Privileged Ones* (Boston: Little, Brown and Company, 1977).

16. Margaret Mead, *Culture and Commitment: A Study of the Generation Gap.* (Garden City, NY: Doubleday, 1970).

17. David Nasaw, *Children in the City. (*New York: Oxford University Press, 1985).

18. John Dewey, *The School and Society* (Chicago: University of Chicago Press, 1900).

19. Martha Wolfenstein and Gilbert Kilman, *Children and the Death of a President* (Garden City, New York: (Doubleday and Company, Inc., 1965).

20. Neil Postman, *Amusing Ourselves to Death* (New York: Viking, 1985) and Joshua Meyrowitz, *No Sense of Place* (New York: Oxford University Press, 1985).

21. Joel Spring, *Educating the Consumer-Citizen: A History of the Marriage of School, Advertising and Media* (Mahwah, N.J.: Lawrence Erlbaum Associates, 2003).

22. Joe McGinnis, *The Selling of the President, 1969* (New York: Trident Press, 1969).

23. Roy Fox, *Harvesting Minds: How TV Commercials Control Kids.* (Westport, Conn: Praeger, 1996).

24. Benjamin Barber, *An Aristocracy of Everyone* (New York: Oxford University Press, 1992) and Robert Dahl, *After the Revolution* (New Haven, Conn.: Yale University Press, 1970).

25. George Kelly, *Theory of Personality* (New York: W.W. Norton and Company, Inc., 1963).

26. Lawrence Grossberg, *Caught in the Crossfire: Kids, Politics and America's Future* (Boulder, Colo.: Paradigm Publishers, 2005) and Karen Sternheimer, *It's Not the Media* (Boulder, Colo.: Westview, 2003).

27. David Buckingham, *The Making of Citizens: Young People, News and Politics* (London, Routledge, 2003).

28. Ron Susskind, "Without a Doubt," *New York Times,* 17, October 2004, 44 (10)

29. Heilbroner, "The Human Prospect," 30.

30. "The First Epistle of Paul the Apostle to the Corinthians," *St James Bible* 1611, 13:9-13.

31. Alice Miller, *For Your Own Good,* translated by Hildegarde and Hunter Hannum (New York: Farrar, Strause, Giroux, 1983).

32. Sigmund Freud, *Civilization and Its Discontents,* translated by James Strachey, (New York: W.W. Norton, c 1961).

33. Glen H. Elder Jr., *Children of the Great Depression: Social Change in Life Experience* (Chicago: University of Chicago Press, 1974).

34. Erikson, *Childhood and Society.*

35. Neil Postman, *The Disappearance of Childhood* (New York: Random House, 1983).

36. Elliott West, *Growing Up With the Country* (Albuquerque, N. Mex.: University of New Mexico Press, 1989).

37. Sylvia Ann Hewlett, *When The Bough Breaks* (New York: Basic Books, 1991) and Allison James and Alan Prout, eds, *Constructing and Reconstructing Childhood: Contemporary Issues in Sociological Study of Childhood* (London: Falmer Press, 1997)

38. Nick Lee, *Childhood and Society: Growing Up in an Age of Uncertainty* (Buckingham, England and Philadelphia: Open University Press, 2001).

39. Jean Baudrillard, *Simulations* (New York: Semiotext(e), 1983).

40. Urie Bronfenbrenner, *The Ecology of Human Development* (Cambridge, Mass. and London: Harvard University Press, 1979).

41. Mary F. Rogers, *Barbie Culture* (Thousand Oaks, Calif.: Sage Publications, 1999) Elizabeth Chinn, *Purchasing Power: Black Kids and Consumer Culture* (Minneapolis: University of Minnesota Press, 2002) and Mary Hilton, ed., *Potent Fictions: Children's Literacy and the Challenge of Popular Culture* (New York and London: Routledge, 1996).

42. Jane M. Healy, *Endangered Minds: Why Children Don't Think and What We Can Do About It* (New York: Simon and Schuster, 1990) and Neil Postman, *Amusing Ourselves to Death* (New York: Viking, 1985).

43. Margaret Mead, *Culture and Commitment A Study of the Generation Gap* (Garden City, N.Y.: Doubleday, 1970).

44. Neil Howe and William Strauss, *Millenials Rising* (New York: Vintage Books, 2000).

45. Gareth Matthews, *Philosophy and the Young Child* (Cambridge, Mass.: Harvard University Press, 1982).

46. Carol Gilligan, *In a Different Voice* (Cambridge, Mass.: Harvard University Press, 1982).

Chapter Two

The Beginnings of the Study

The historical and social forces that lead to a study of children at any particular time are complex and hover over the methods, results and interpretations that emerge. As the experiences of children and our ideas about them change, listening to some of their voices provides information that can be useful. The interviews and surveys in this particular study occurred at five different time periods. The first set of interviews in 1995 was a cross sectional discussion with children about images of power offered by the media. The next three sets of interviews took place during the 1996, 2000 and 2004 elections. The last set took place in the fall of 2005, not an election year. The last four of the investigations included surveys as well as interviews. Covering a ten- year span, these reflections by children offer a glimpse into the changing political scene and some children's reactions to it.

The significance of any study depends on its parameters. As a state in the northeastern part of the country, Vermont has certain liberal traditions that have co-existed with its generally Republican voting history. Vermont is a poor state and the community in which this study took place is one of its poorest as evidenced by the percentage of children on free and reduced price lunches as well as the high unemployment rate. Despite this, the community boasts two residential colleges, a community college, a medical center, a mental health center, a museum, an Equity theatre company and in the adjoining town, another museum and a volunteer symphony orchestra as well as an arts center.

The town seems never to have recovered from being a failed textile center and the large mill that once supplied the employment for the people now houses a variety of enterprises from a fitness center to a bicycle store and some small businesses. Like many small New England towns, megastores such as Wal-Mart and Home Depot and franchise food places such as Dunkin' Donuts, McDonald's and Wendy's have transformed the farmland on the outskirts of Main Street into a conventional strip development. The wealth in the county lies to the North in more rural towns.

The children who were interviewed are from a lower middle to middle income class. They are not from the school that serves two low-income housing developments or from the school that is in the wealthier section of town. In the four outlying communities in the supervisory union, there is only one school for each community. This might, therefore, suggest more diversity in those schools. However, there are four private schools in the community that siphon off particular populations. There is a Protestant Christian school, a Roman Catholic school and two progressive schools that take from all of the public school populations those whose parents have clearly defined ideas what they want for their children's education. As in the rest of the state, there also is a sizable number of home schooled children.

The children who were surveyed come from all four of the public schools in the district, plus two of the schools in the outlying communities. All of the schools in the supervisory union feed into a single middle school and a secondary school. The middle school consists of grades seven and eight. There has been controversy about sending sixth graders to the middle school.

The community is predominately white, as is the state. Like the state, however, the town has seen a gradual increase in its non-white population; some of it the result of international adoptions, some of it from an immigration of Asian families, displaced by conflicts in their home countries and welcomed into the state more easily than the few African Americans. Still, the state is 96 percent white and the Vermont schools in this study range from 95 percent to 99 percent white. Therefore, many of the children's views about minorities are based on information that they have received from books, movies and television.

After the first year, the children in the interviews and surveys were all sixth graders. Other than the fact that the interviewed children came from the same school and had been selected as a representative sample of their class, other information about the children only emerged in the course of the interviews. I never knew any of the children's last names or any family or school history. All of the interviewed children had their parents' permission to take part in the study. The teachers distributed and kept the parental permission forms. There were four boys and four girls in each interviewed group. The surveyed children were also not identified except by age, gender, grade and school.

In all of the interviews, the focus was on politics and the media. These were the topics that the parents were informed would be discussed. Therefore, there were many areas that were excluded or only touched on briefly as the children raised them. Everything that the children said was accepted. There was no attempt to find out the specific political affiliations of the children or their families. Questions were general to allow the most flexibility for the children to express their views. Follow-up questions were usually for clarification or for explanations of why the children thought as they did. Other than asking questions, the researcher only offered factual corrections when necessary or definitions as the children asked for them. Her role was not that of a teacher and she placed no value judgements on the children's perspectives.

Sixth graders are at a crossroads in their development. They have the verbal and cognitive skills necessary for analyzing social phenomena. According to Piaget, most of them are moving into the stage of formal operations where they are capable of formal thinking about abstract phenomena such as justice, freedom and democracy. Sixth graders are also moving out of the so-called latency period towards sexual maturity. Not yet in the throes of adolescence, sixth graders have mastered many of the tasks society, through its schools, requires of them. Developmentally, sixth-graders are articulate about their views and are concerned about issues of justice and fairness, important concepts in democratic elections.

For the final study, there was an attempt to interview and survey an urban population to contrast some of the views that might have resulted from the particular rural environment in which the original study children grow up. However, this was difficult. Making contact to conduct surveys, much less set up interviews was complex. Understandably, schools have procedures to protect children, but even getting access to the procedures was a challenge. Therefore, only two schools in a nearby urban area were available for surveys. Although by the distribution of ethnicity in their own state, these schools were heavily Caucasian, 74 percent and 84 percent. Compared to the Vermont communities, they offered far more diversity. Surveys were also distributed to a middle-income suburban school in Massachusetts. This was a predominately white community (89.12 percent) with only 3.3 percent of the population in the community below the poverty line.[1]

In all of the election studies, the children were interviewed each week for six to seven weeks from September through November. For the non-election year study, the interviewer met with the children for seven weeks in the fall and two weeks in January. All of the interviews were taped. The benefit of meeting with the same informants over a period of time is that the strength of their views can be assessed. Children, like adults, have varying opinions on the same topic that can be influenced by additional information. Ideas and beliefs can be clarified through ongoing discussions.

The surveys in the subsequent studies were distributed during the same time period. The interviews usually took place in the school library or in an art classroom. When the venue changed, sometimes to another classroom or the gymnasium, the change was reflected in the change in the students' behaviors. This was most evident in the 1996 study when a meeting took place in the gymnasium. For the most part, the interviews were conducted in a room without other adults. When another adult was present, she was quietly working in another part of the room or library.

The sessions were usually forty-five minutes to an hour long and in the mornings. Children rarely missed any of the sessions. During the four studies in the same school, there were two different teachers who cooperated with the study. Both of them were generous in their support, but beyond selecting the children and the spaces, they allowed the interviewer complete freedom. The researcher did share the papers written about the studies with all of the schools that participated in the surveys and the interviews.

The first sixth grade teacher selected the children in order to provide a cross section of the children in her class. They were from a range of socioeconomic backgrounds. They were all children who liked each other and whom, the teacher said, basically had positive attitudes towards school. She gave me brief sketches of the children and where she thought they were in the level of their thinking. She indicated that the four boys and one of the girls were in transition to a more abstract stage. She did not however discuss anything about their school performance or family situations. One of the few black children in the school was in the group.

With the first group, the teacher also provided a general idea of what she was doing in class in terms of current events. Each Wednesday the class had a town meeting for solving problems and for celebrating the children's accomplishments. Except for checking in and clarifying some information about a film shown in class, the interviews were conducted independently of the teacher. This was important for one of the children who, sometimes before she spoke, would ask, "Who's going to listen to these tapes?" Children were always assured that their teachers would not hear the tapes although they never said anything that was inappropriate. Their criticisms of their education were usually general and descriptive of a frustration with methods and not individuals.

This was also important to the children in the other studies. They understood that they would not be able to be identified. The second teacher was also helpful in his selection of the children, although without providing as much background information. These children were also a cross-section. They were also from two different sixth-grade classrooms. He also suggested a follow-up meeting in May with the 2004 group, which was quite informative.

This chapter will provide a report of the first cross sectional study that was the impetus for the subsequent studies. In the next two chapters the other studies and the surveys will be examined.

Politics is depicted both directly and indirectly in the media. Films and television programs that deal overtly with the issues of democracy are usually clear about the issues. *All the King's Men, The Candidate, The Manchurian Candidate, Wag the Dog* as films and *The West Wing* as a television program are among the examples provided to children and adults that provide civic lessons in the guise of entertainment. However, other depictions of power and authority also teach children about the political life they will inherit.

Interviewing a cross section of children in 1995 demonstrates how persistent some of these images are as well as the changes that occur among different cohorts of children. The informants in this study consisted of five-year-olds in a campus-based college preschool, two groups of public school third graders and two groups of sixth graders from a different public school.

The children were interviewed in groups, following Buckingham's model[2] on the assumption that the interaction among the children provides a more complex picture of children's viewing. In a group, the power of the interviewer is mitigated. This was certainly true with these children. Starting with a set of questions that were the same for each group; further questions built on the children's responses. No teacher was present for the interviews except with the group of five-year olds.

With the public school groups, some of the follow up questions were also the same. All of the groups were asked *What is power? Who has power? Do you know anyone who has power? Who is powerful in tv and the movies? What makes them powerful? Who has the power to make rules? What kind of rules are there? Who has to follow the rules? How do they get people to follow rules? What if rules aren't followed? Who in television and the movies has the power to make rules?*

The third and sixth graders, were also asked *How do movies and television make you think about people you don't know? Do you have rules about what movies and television you can watch? Are there some movies children should not see? What movies would you tell an adult to watch if they wanted to learn about power?*

Talking with children is an enlightening experience. They are thoughtful and cooperative respondents. The group dynamics worked extremely well as the children listened to each other, modifying and expanding on each other's responses. Except for the last group of sixth graders, there were consistent gender differences in views of television and movies, with girls generally eschewing violent movies. The differences between the last group of girls and the others was not so much that they liked violence in movies as much as there was a greater cynicism about politics and about the amount of violence in the world in which children live.

Children in all groups and at all ages had a clear sense of television and movies as separate from reality. The first response in all the groups, including the five-year olds, as to who had power to make rules in the movies, was "the director." When asked to define power, the five-year-olds initially thought concretely and the first answer was "something that generates electricity." After a string of answers that focused on lights and machines, a child said, "God," and the direction changed to include Santa, angels and Cupid. Once the question was raised as to who had power in television and the movies, the children had a long list which included every superhero on television and in the movies for the past five years, such is the impact of reruns and VCRs. One five year old girl cited the X-Men, noting that she was not allowed to watch it at home, but had seen it at a friend's house. After a long list of powerful men, one girl said quietly, "Barney. The power of love and caring." The kindergarten teacher, who was the only teacher present at any of the interviews because of the age of the children, countered the derisive hoots from the five-year-old boys. She stopped the discussion to remind the group that they had to respect each other's opinions.

At a subsequent discussion with the kindergartners, some of the girls objected to the fact that most of the powerful people named were men and they generated some female names like Wonder Woman and She-Ra. This division between boys and girls views was most evident among the third graders.

In the third grade groups the girls generally disliked violent movies in contrast to the boys. These groups were the ones who thought that the V-chip was a good idea. Like the sixth graders they cited Beavis and Butthead as a bad influence on younger children. The children were clear that there should be rules based on age. "It all depends on the age, I think. Like older kids can watch more violent movies or shows or anything." The children also felt that the morals at the end of programs were effective for most children, but were concerned about children who could not read the messages or who did not pay attention to them. "Well if they are like little kids, they should have lots of rules, like not watching videos that are smoking or hitting or punching, but if they are like us, I don't know. I don't think we should have any rules because we understand most everything." This response is consistent with most studies that show people concerned with the impact of the media on other people, but not on them.

For the third graders, swearing was as worrisome a model as physical violence and they spent as much time as any concerned censor wondering how many swear words were acceptable and in what context. "If it has one or two swear words, like one, and you like the show . . . I think if you take the advice from it you should be able to watch. If you don't take the advice from it, the parents shouldn't let them see it."

The children were clear that movies, television and computers had an impact on children's behavior. "Sometimes bad movies encourage bad people to be bad." noted a third grader. A sixth grader's observation that, "I'm not the kind of person who will get a gun because Sylvester Stallone has one." was countered by, "If someone has no power or low self esteem they might."

In discussing computers before the widespread availability of video games, the third graders had mixed feelings about games on computers as opposed to educational software. They were also aware of the issues of violence that concerned adults about computer games.

"I think if computers were only for learning, no one would want to use them because they wouldn't be any fun."

"Learning can be fun, but wouldn't someone get bored with always math, always reading, always . . ."

"I don't think that it is right because *Carmen Sandiego* is fun and you can learn all different places."

"Imagine any games on computers and there were not—and all computers were learning it would get boring at a certain point"

"It would be like only having one disk. Always doing one thing. Just learning disks."

"I guess, but there is like this math disk you have to shoot up in the air to get the answer . . ."

"Like a game. It's a game. You are not really hurting or shooting anyone. You are doing it on something that's not a person. You are just doing it with a gun."

Children were aware that movies were not always accurate in telling them about people that they did not know personally. Both third graders and sixth graders felt that cities were not as bad as depicted on television. As a sixth grader observed, "Like *Dangerous Minds*, they really showed how bad the city is, but there are some spots in the city that are not all that bad. If you watch this movie, you get an idea about what cities are like, but not all cities are like that."

The sixth graders discussed the function of violence as part of the action of a movie or television program. One-sixth grade girl who noted that there was violence in real life also commented gently, "If you take out the violence, (from movies) you don't have the villain, and if you don't have a villain, you don't have a good guy." Some sixth graders noted that if violence were removed from the movies, children would find it in books.

Still the media did induce anxiety as one third-grade girl indicated when responding to the question about what rules one learned from watching videos and television. "You always have to lock the doors and close the windows when you leave the house so no one breaks in and not to run away from home because on tv it showed someone who ran away from home and someone shot him"

In discussing violence, both third and sixth graders noted that there was violence in the community where they lived. Automobile accidents, vandalism and local fights were cited as examples. Sixth graders were particularly upset that adults did not enforce rules more effectively. They talked about being able to see R rated movies in Cineplexes by buying tickets for one movie and going into another. Children being able to buy cigarettes also upset them. They felt that laws were not enforced. When asked what movies and television taught them about the police, they replied that the police were corrupt and cited Mark Furhman as an example. In talking about the O. J. Simpson trial, they made it clear that they felt that he was acquitted because he had money. Power and money, the sixth graders claimed, were similar. "The way it is now you don't see any homeless man with power. All you can see is a man with money. That's how it is."

In all of the groups the children cited the president as someone with power to make the rules, but the discussion among the sixth graders, not surprisingly, was more detailed. When they could vote, they said they would want a person who was smart, fair, had proved that he or she was good for the job and was not in it for the money. The children felt that wars were all about money. The anti-war sentiment that the children felt was revealed at a number of points. When discussing what was the most important thing a president could do for the country, not sending men to war was most frequently mentioned.

One sixth-grade boy said, "What gets me . . . that when they go to the Vietnam war, it is the government's choice and they pick people, they picked young people and they didn't even want to go, but they made them or they'd get arrested. That's not very nice"

One group of sixth graders was particularly upset about the President's suggestion that children wear uniforms to school. "The President said that if kids from kindergarten to sixth grade wore uniforms they would not get violent. More kids would get violent."

"Go to a private school. This is a public school."

"Who wants to wear a dress every single day?"

"We would go on strike." Clearly, the children felt that changing clothes was not going to do much to stop violence and that their rights would be infringed. However, in the discussion with all of the groups, the rules and regula-tions that their parents used to restrict their viewing of movies and television were accepted as appropriate, and just. In some cases children noted that they did not follow all of their parents rules about running in the house or beating up on their little brothers and sisters, but whether followed or not, parental limita-tions about media viewing were seen favorably. The amount of control the par-ents exercised was more lenient as the children got older so this may be why each group felt comfortable with parental strictures. There is also the possibility that the children were providing socially approved responses to the interviewer. However, when I said at one point to a third grade group, "I'm getting the idea that none of you ever watches anything with violence in it," they quickly told me I was getting the wrong idea.

Ambivalence about authority was evident in all of the discussions. Once beyond the circle of their families, children were suspicious of the information that they got from television, news and the movies. Perhaps this skepticism is healthy, but perhaps it leads to a sense of powerlessness. What are children who say the following learning about politics?

"They all just talk and they get president, they sit back and don't do any-thing."

"Most of the presidents when they get elected they don't do what they said they were going to do."

"Some of the movies I watch are about the government hiding stuff about aliens and stuff and that really makes me think a lot. What if the government is really hiding stuff about that? What would you do? Would you try to make friends with aliens?"

The children talked about one program specifically. "My brother used to watch *Power Rangers* and they taught him to start punching and kicking and hurting people, so my Mom said he couldn't watch anymore." Other children said that they learned more than that because the program said that karate was about discipline and control. Another child started training in martial arts be-cause of his interest in *Power Rangers*.

All of this conversation has to be put in context. Children have developed the vocabulary of the talk shows. The format of my inquiry was a familiar one and they responded with the ease and sophistication of seasoned viewers en-lightening a naive and unwary researcher on the customs and values of the country. If, however, as Barber[3] says, that education for democracy means the telling of a national story in which there is the "victory of aspiration over his-tory," one is troubled by the statement, "Like the Civil War didn't make any sense either because eventually they are just all going to come together any-way." Is this sixth grader talking about a major political event in the nation's history or about the outcome of another television special?

Taking the advice of my informants about which media texts I should study, I examined four episodes of *Power Rangers*, the movies *Toy Story* and *In the Line of Fire* as representative of movies and television watched and recom-mended by the different age groups.

Watching videos of *Power Rangers* is probably a different experience than watching the program on television. "It's big, It's bold, It's the next action step in adventure packed, live action children's programming." This is the advertisement for *VR Troopers* which precedes each episode, along with advertisements for the Power Ranger Fan Club. There is also a segment in which the Power Rangers are interviewed in auditoriums filled with children. The Ranger featured on the video takes the lead in these interviews which are intercut with a studio interview. Wholesome messages about teamwork abound, as do explanations about the programs. Power Rangers really don't get hurt in their fights. "What we do is fantasy," proclaims Kimberly the Pink Ranger. Then the episode begins with its "Go, Go, Power Rangers" song while the name and face of each actor is paired with their Power Ranger image.

As in most superhero fantasies, the identity of the Power Rangers is unknown to the general population although the villains whose purpose it is to conquer earth know them. These all-American teen-agers become Power Rangers by holding up their insignias representing beasts such as mastodon, pterodactyl, triceratops, tyrannosaurus and saber tooth tiger and, by invoking their power, are transformed into Power Rangers with suits of different colors. Their animals are actually Dinozords, mechanical beasts, which under the proper incantation become a huge transformer, the Megazord, into which the Power Rangers fly when their karate actions are not sufficient to save the day. This necessity occurs in every episode.

The master villain is Rita Repulsa who had been imprisoned for ten thousand years, but is now free to conquer the earth. She is Asian, wearing a huge medieval type costume and hissing her commands in obviously dubbed speech. Many of her henchmen are ridiculous figures, costumed like sci-fi characters. Their acting is broad to say the least. Perhaps the exaggerated costumes require their exaggerated speech. Or perhaps it is the juxtaposition of the Japanese and American elements in the program. The comic element is echoed in the figures of Bulk and Skull in the high school context. They are leather-jacketed bullies who are always trying to intimidate the heroes and heroines in their non-Power Ranger identities. However, early in each episode they are foiled. Then the plot begins with some new challenge from Rita. She is continuously developing new warriors to attack the Power Rangers. The Power Rangers must never use their powers for their own gain and they must never increase the level of the battle unless provoked by Rita. This wicked mother figure is balanced by Zord, the head of a male, who appears in the central computer control power station. Assisted by Alpha, a robot and another humorous figure, Zord provides whatever counter-balancing assistance the Power Rangers need in their fight to preserve the planet.

Two of the six Power Rangers are women. One of them is Asian American and one of the male Rangers is an African American, thereby achieving the proper mixture for a contemporary team of superheroes. In their high school lives, the Rangers usually appear in school by their lockers where they often have to deal with the petty harassment of Bulk and Skull. Otherwise, their lives are trouble free with minor concerns such as a surprise birthday party. Underneath this surface, however, lurks the on-going danger to the earth on the part of the villains. The alien nature of these creatures makes one think of the sixth grader who said that he didn't like to think of aliens because he dreamed he might be abducted. In Power Rangers we do see the two worlds, even if to adult eyes the aliens are figures of ridicule rather than of threat. Except for Zord, who is disembodied authority, there are few other adults present in the lives of the Rangers. The terrain of battle is itself alien as there are explosions and conflicts between the large creatures that stomp on the earth and crush cities. Although in one episode some teen-agers are watching the alien attack on television where it supposedly is a news broadcast, the immediate environment in which people live seems undisturbed by the struggles. Perhaps, it is far-fetched to see in these images the picture of a suburban America undisturbed by the battles and dangers and the destruction of cities in other countries.

Child viewers from five onward see the teamwork of the Rangers as one of the dominant elements in the program. In the minimal plot of the high school story the Rangers plan parties, baby-sit and generally act as media adolescents. This reinforces their role as helpers. Much is made of using power for good, just as the United States is convinced it always uses its power for good. Most of the conflicts are stylized karate exercises with some swordplay. None of the humans do more than tumble, fall, roll over and leap, although there are flashes of light zapping people and animating swords. The most intense conflict is that between the machines. Enemies are inhuman except for the excessively evil Rita. The dullness of the main characters contrasts with the explosions, lights, and sounds of the fights. This sense of conflict lurking beneath the surface of placidity haunts the program like a surrealist's dream. Seeing Kimberley kicking and chopping at the putty men with her little purse around her neck before her body morphs into its pink Ranger guise is a metaphor of feminist power to enchant the minds of five year old girls, if that is indeed the power they want.

Listening to the children suggests that these images may present conflicting ideas. The appeal of secret identities concealing hidden powers has appeal as the superhero genre demonstrates. Yet the repetitive threat that is also omnipresent may too accurately reflect the threat that the media promises is lurking everywhere.

When we think of power, we must also consider powerlessness and what is more powerless than a child, but a child's toy. The pleasures of *Toy Story* are such that one is tempted to follow the lead of the sixth grader who said, "I don't pay any attention to the message. I just watch the movie."

One of the sad lessons Buzz Lightyear must learn is that he is only a toy. This information almost destroys him. Toys owe their lives and personality and reality to the ability of children to transform them. Andy and Sid are two sides of the same powerful entity; one of whom destroys by his mutilation of toys and the other by his indifference. Andy is always losing or misplacing his toys.

The playroom is a colony of vulnerable toys, seeking to maintain the favor of a careless master. Woody demonstrates leadership by rallying the toys to action. His plans, however, often do not succeed. Deploying the troop of little green soldiers to spy on the humans is the act of a subjected and weakened group. Woody has many of the characteristics of the mythic Western hero. Courage, tenacity and ingenuity are his weapons. The cowboy and the astronaut are the American ideals of manhood; both challenging the frontiers of space. In reality, however, their achievements are accidental as when Buzz seems to be able to fly as he claims. Assured of his own reality, Buzz struts proudly, unwilling to accept his status. When he sees himself advertised on television, the media shatters Buzz's illusions about himself and renders him incapable of action.

The rebellion of the despised is what saves Buzz. The toys who have been transformed by Sid's technology so that they are mutants, lead the revolution while the nice, middle-class toys are relatively helpless, unable to organize themselves. Teamwork, which is so often stressed in films for children again is demonstrated as the most effective way to succeed even though the two protagonists are the masculine icons of rugged individualism, Woody representing the past and Buzz the technological future. At the movie's end, the soldiers are sent on another reconnaissance mission to discover what new threat there is to the toys that live precariously in Andy's favor.

Since the third graders recommended this movie, I have tried to fathom what they wished to tell me. One can see this movie as a parable of sibling rivalry or one can see it as an image of the weak dependent upon the powerful. Only the toys who are completely mistreated by Sid are capable of striking back. The other toys must wait. The unexpected can change the toys' lives precipitously. They can be packed up or left behind. They are silent except among themselves. Victory is temporary as they wait to find out what the presence of a dog in the house will do to their status. Although the toys live in a relatively safe and pleasant environment, they have little control over their fate.

In the Line of Fire is a political movie about the attempted assassination of a President. Several of the sixth graders noted that movies about Presidents usually involved them being killed. One of the movie's most vivid images is of the secret service men hustling the President from the banquet room, through the kitchen, and into a car. For adults the kitchen brings back memories of Robert Kennedy; for the children the headlong race has its own internal dynamic suggesting the danger and the panic in an unstable world. Although this moment has been anticipated from the first line of the movie by Frank Horrigan's partner, "I'm going to get killed," he says as he arrive late to their assignment, the rapidity of the action increases rather than releases tension.

One of the themes in this movie, which is not foreign to children used to the shifting identities of Power Rangers and other comic book and television heroes, is the relationship between the hero and the villain. Not only does Mitch Leary, the villain, insist on the relationship between them, but the film continually provides parallels in their unsuccessful marriages, their problems with the authorities within their own organizations and the confidence and coolness with which they act. Each is willing to give up his life, one to save the President and one to kill him. The scenes in which each holds the other's life in his hand emphasizes their oneness.

The setting of the movie in Washington with its landmarks familiar to children from other movies and from their textbooks and, for some, from trips, enhances the sense of a story that could happen. The photographs of John Kennedy's assassination, with a young Clint Eastwood in the background, mixes realities so that the pretend story vibrates with paranoid possibilities. We see the trappings of power in the secret service men around the President, but even here we are told it is fake within a fake. The panting Secret Service men around the car are not really necessary because the car is built like a tank.

The convoluted nature of relationships and identities is played out over and over again. Frank and his partner pretending to be criminals, Frank pretending to shoot his partner. Would he have really killed him? The CIA does not give the Secret Service men the information they need about a former CIA agent, an agent gone bad. Two women are killed because one accidentally reveals knowledge she did not know was lethal. The twists and turns make the plot more involving, but they also build up a world of distrust and danger

Besides learning how to build a plastic gun and store bullets so that they will get past a metal detector, children see the deceptions and the petty jealousies that make it difficult for the hero to do his job. In the climatic scene we have Frank supposedly talking to Mitch, but really instructing the Secret Service. According to his own code and still in control, Mitch lets go of Frank's hand and drops to his death. But like the villain in a children's cartoon, Mitch's voice, via the technology of the answering machine, continues to challenge Frank.

Although much is made of the fact that one of the Secret Service agents is a woman, this is a film about the relationship between pairs of men, Frank and his partner, Frank and Mitch. The homoerotic overtones in Mitch's relationship to Frank is made explicit when Mitch takes Frank's gun into his mouth in the rooftop scene. Mitch then kills his rival, Frank's partner. Power is masculine in this political adventure. The woman is the man's prize at the end of the struggle for dominance among men.

After reviewing these films and videos and listening to the children, what have we learned about the relationship between the media and children's ideas about politics? Certainly, there is confirmation of the extensive research findings which say that television and movies create a world which is frightening and that we probably have to worry more about apathy than violence as children feel overwhelmed by the action which they see depicted. However, despite the violence they watch, or perhaps because of it, they are not supportive of the idea of Presidents sending Americans to war. Nor do they generally think highly of Presidents or other politicians. If as Hess and Torney claimed in 1967[4] children's first identification with government is through the President, this deterioration from the positive regard in which children held the Presidency should be a matter of some concern.

Children have learned not to believe what they are told on television; not all the bad stuff about people and places with which they are not familiar and not much good stuff either. These children are suspicious of their government. Movies such as *In the Line of Fire* reinforce this attitude.

Perhaps there is more control of television and movie viewing on the part of parents for these particular groups of children than might have been anticipated. Children appreciate consistency in the setting and maintaining of rules. They also articulate a developmental point of view in terms of the limits that should be set for television viewing.

The idea of an informed citizenry who will make our democratic institutions effective because decisions will be wisely made by people with shared values is an idea that predates contemporary technology. Edward Murrow saw television as providing "the greatest classroom in the world." However, it seems to be a classroom in which the teachers are often absent, leaving the children to learn their own lessons.

Notes

1.<http://www.schoolreview.com/county_elementary_schools/stateid/VT/count<y50 003>1/26/2006),<http://new-york.schooltree.org/public/Rennsselaer-Middle-061750.html > (1/26/2006) and (11/23/2005) <http:??en.wikipedia.org/wiki/Shrewsbury, Massachu-setts>(11/23/2005)
<htttp://ny.localschooldirectory.com/schools_info.php/school_id/61398> (11/23/2005

2. David Buckingham, *Children Talking Television.* (London: The Falmer Press, 1993).

3. Benjamin R. Barber, *An Aristocracy of Everyone.* (New York: Oxford University Press, 1992).

4. Robert D. Hess and Judith V. Torney. *The Development of Political Attitudes in Children.* (Garden City, New York: Doubleday and Co., 1967).

Chapter Three

A Look at Three Elections

The first of the studies in which children were interviewed over a period of six weeks about the presidential election took place in 1996. The teacher selected the children to provide a cross section from her class. There were four boys and four girls. One of the boys was African American. The information from this study can be divided into three parts. The children's specific views about politics and the election process, the issues about education which the children raised and which were far more important to them than the questions asked of them, and observations of the children and their interactions.

The children knew who the candidates for president and vice president were as well as who was the governor in the state. They did not know who was running against the governor, but in that they were not much different from many adults in a state where the governor had a 70 percent approval rating and a political unknown for an opponent.

When asked what the president does, the responses were: "He runs the country and helps out with everything like the Saddam Hussein and sends soldiers over there"

"Doesn't he like make laws and make sure, he approves of them after they are written?"

"He takes care of the world. He makes sure that all the schools are right and everything like that."

Then Stacey, the African American boy said, "I think ever since President Clinton has been elected, there has been a lot of changes. I used to live in Florida. When George Bush was president there was a lot more gang fights going on. When President Clinton got elected, the first day that he was elected I saw a police car go by my house. They made a drug bust. He made a big change for me when he got elected president of the United States"

Matt, one of the other boys, said, "One of the reasons that I'm pretty sure that I want Bill Clinton to win . . . because he is really giving a crackdown on smoking. There can't be any smoking logos at sporting events because they might show up on camera and that would be an ad. He is giving fines to clerks that are giving people under twenty-one cigarettes. That's why I want him to win"

Stacey picked up on this and said, "I'd like to relate to what Matt said. Like if a clerk in Bennington sold cigarettes to somebody under twenty-one, he made a law that they would get their license taken away and that's already happened, I believe, to two people in Bennington, Mrs Clark told us. I think that's a very good law"

All the other students agreed and said they didn't smoke and recounted stories of trying to get their parents to stop smoking. Drugs, crime and pollution were important issues for them. Although in later sessions they would add poverty, racism, war and child abuse to this list, the issues to which they kept returning were these. A videotaped film the teacher showed them in which children questioned President Clinton about what he had accomplished impressed them. They did not see any similar tape about Bob Dole. When Mrs. Clark was asked about what seemed to be an imbalance in presentation, she explained that the videotape was not a campaign one and that the focus was on the children asking questions of the president and not on the president. That may have been the intent, but the effect on the children was to present Clinton as an effective president who had created changes in response to the concerns of children.

Although the children live in a state that is rated to be one of the safest in the nation, they expressed anxiety about drugs and crime, reporting incidents where their families' or friends' homes had been burglarized. All of the children had taken part in the DARE program and thought it was effective. "They made it fun to learn."

"It's cool, because it teaches you about drugs and not to use them." The children were unanimous in believing that a woman would make a good president. One of the boys said a woman ". . . could kick Bill Clinton's butt in an election because some people are getting tired of guy presidents."

A girl said, "Some women have different ideas and they would try really hard to fight for what they believe in and have things be fair." The boys rejected the idea that women were smarter, but they agreed that a woman could lead the nation into war if necessary although they thought it was more likely that women would work harder for peace than a man would. One girl thought that a woman president would make abortion illegal because men did not know what it was like to be a mom.

As they discussed the issue further, there were many "it depends" statements as they recognized that individuals and situations affected who should be president. However, all of the children remained committed throughout the sessions to the feasibility and desirability of a woman candidate for president.

The major source for their ideas about politics seemed to come from the school. They said that they did not often discuss politics with their parents although they were clear as to whom their parents supported. They also felt, however, that they should hold their own ideas, independent of their parents. They got most of their information from watching the news on television, although the girls generally said they did not watch very often. The news was perceived as being unfair to all the candidates. "Making candidates look bad makes it unfair to them and the people." In terms of television political campaign ads, they said that candidates should just say what they would do and not attack each other. The suggestion was made that any money left over from presidential campaigns should be given to poor people.

One part of the political process that the children observed on television was the nominating convention that they all agreed was boring, whether Democratic or Republican. They saw a political party as ". . . a bunch of these old people who get together and talk and sit there and eat." Sharon had seen part of the locally televised selectmen's meeting and had recognized parents of some of her friends. "All they do is sit around a table and talk and that's called a party. I don't think so."

Although the school was seen as providing most of the students' information about government, the children felt that there was not much discussion about issues such as racism. They also did not discuss racism with their parents. This might not be surprising in a state with a minute African American population, but as they all acknowledged they had friends who were black, including Stacey who was sitting at the table. They made it clear that they were not prejudiced and did not approve of prejudice. To some degree, they were criticizing the teaching around this topic, but also protesting the need to deal with it. "It's not something that sticks in our heads."

"It's boring."

"It's what we already know."

"It's for grown-ups. We shouldn't have to worry about it because we're not eighteen yet. We're kids" This theme of being "kids" and not having to be concerned about social issues was reiterated frequently by the girls.

Matt, on the other hand, when asked what advice to give to President Clinton, said, "Pay attention to kids more. We are the next generation. We're going to have to run this country once in a while. Maybe not us in particular, but some one of these kids"

The influence of parents was not as direct in terms of politics as it was in terms of ethics and morality. When asked what they would do if a friend stole a book, Brad responded, "First of all, they wouldn't steal a book. They would steal something better."

When all agreed that a CD was better, they all indicated that they would have their friends return it. They then told stories of thefts in which parents' reactions were crucial. The parents grounded children who stole and made them repay anything that was due. The children told how parents taught them about honesty and responsibility. This line of inquiry was geared to arrive at the issue of good citizenship. Andrew said that the way you taught someone to be a good citizen was to be a good citizen. From their accounts it was easy to see that their parents played that role in their lives, by clearly letting them know what was right and wrong and the consequences for negative behavior and by the model of citizenship they provided.

In response to these and other questions, the children shared their knowledge and understanding about taxes, social problems and the politicians who they hoped would give greater financial support to schools. They saw the political process as generally fair and politicians as working to solve the country's problems. Their views leaned toward the liberal except on the issue of crime that they thought should be strongly punished. They wanted to see criminals locked up for long periods. They generally advocated laws that would control what people did in the areas of drugs, smoking and pollution. They were committed to equality between the sexes and the races. The influence that the media seemed to have was not specific to political campaigns or candidates, but to an atmosphere of potential danger from a complex society.

The politics the children were most interested in, however, was the politics of the school where they felt disenfranchised. "They ask for our opinions, but they don't even listen to our opinions." Throughout the sessions, but particularly in the two that were situated in other than the usual location, the children raised issues that concerned them intensely. They felt that they were not being educationally challenged. Much of the material they were learning, they already knew. They also felt that they did not get the help they needed when they did not know something. They talked about math challenge homework which they did not understand and which they were expected to solve themselves. They were particularly upset that they no longer had a recess period that they had last year, but rather a more structured time called intramurals. These complaints were pressed by the girls at first, but the boys agreed and added details.

The children contrasted the teaching techniques of their regular teacher and the male student teacher who they said helped them, made learning fun and didn't yell at them if they didn't know an answer. They wanted more projects and learning to be more fun. They wanted more time to talk to their friends. They objected to having their notes confiscated. "They say we can only talk to the people in front of us and in back of us so we write notes to communicate to other people and they won't let us do it."

When they complained about getting a CRS, and were asked what it was, they explained that the letters stood for the Code of Responsibility for Students. When students did not follow the code, their transgression was written up, hence the acronym.

Ashley included the research project as a part of the system of injustice. They were assigned rather than asked to participate in the weekly interviews. They didn't care about politics. At one point the group turned on Matt as a person who was interested in the project because he read, worked on his computer and watched the news. Stacey called him an "educational freak," leading Matt to protest, "I do not spend all my time educating myself."

Their greatest unhappiness, however, was focused on the children whom they perceived as "bad"; children who had problems learning and who were compensated for their disabilities and bad behaviors by rewards that good kids did not get. They felt that they were being held back educationally by these children who were also not learning. They should "stay them back." One child who combined learning difficulties with behaviors that were threatening to the other children particularly upset them. When he had attacked another child, he was not given a CRS but only a minus on his chart. He was allowed to go swimming while other students no longer have recess. All of the children were angry at those whom they felt prevented them from learning more.

Stacey gave an illuminating analysis of the advantages of being bad. "The bad kids get privileges so I figure I'm always a straight A student. I know how to do my work so I might just as well start being bad. I get privileges. I have two in schools, two out of schools (suspensions), six CRSs. CRS is just a piece of paper. In school is cool because you don't get homework because you never see your teacher. Out of school is even cooler because you get to stay home and watch different tv shows"

What seemed clear was that the children's perceptions and the adults' were quite different. What the school sees as a punishment, Stacey sees as a privilege. The other element is that the standards and expectations are so low that Stacey can see himself as a successful learner even when he misses classes. Although in this particular session, the children were vehement about the children who were not learning, at other times they were sympathetic to the category of children with disabilities.

In their experience, however, the policy of including children with learning problems in their classrooms is an infringement on their right to learn. Both the boys and the girls felt that some of these special children could learn if they tried hard. If these special needs children could not, than they should be held back or sent to resource rooms. However noble the goal of integrating disabled children into a regular classroom, the process, obviously, has to be more carefully monitored to be successful. What the sixth graders missed was seeing negative behavior punished, good behavior rewarded and their classroom learning as stimulating. Whether "good children," which they identified themselves as being, should be rewarded according to Stacey's system or not is debatable. What would they see as a reward for their virtues?

Besides the children's specific responses to the research questions, watching their interactions over time was revealing. The most obvious difference was between the girls and the boys. This was a difference that was surprisingly consistent across all the groups that were interviewed over the years, with the exception of the group interviewed in 2000. In the 1996 group, although they were distinct individuals as Mrs. Clark promised, the contrast between the involvement of the girls and the boys was striking. Matt stood out for his continually thoughtful analysis as did Stacey, but Bradley and Andrew were also engaged with the topic and offered insights and were interested in the project.

The girls, on the other hand, were indifferent or resistant to the project. Ashley was the leader of the girls. She would often start her remarks with, "I have two things to say." She expressed herself primarily through stories as did Sharon and Maddie. Sharon had difficulty staying in her seat while Maddie retreated into "I don't know" or "It's boring"; occasionally delivering valuable commentary.

Ellen said little, becoming more resistant to the project as it went on. When Ellen did speak, her reasoning was more like that of the boys than of the girls. The girls were the ones who kept insisting that they were "kids" and shouldn't have to think about these issues. In her work, Carol Gilligan[1] posits eleven as a crucial turning point for girls in their development. Although girls generally seem more attuned to the climate of elementary school than boys, achieving more prominence than they will in middle and high school, the hesitation with which the girls approached the discussion of politics was evident.

Generally the children were accepting and supportive of each other. Their relationship with Stacey mixed an awareness of his difference with an acceptance of him as an individual. It was the girls, however, who were most resistant to the authority of the researcher. Challenging authority on a personal level seemed more comfortable for them than challenging it intellectually or abstractly in a discussion of issues.

Although at times most of them had difficulty listening to each other and taking turns, the girls were usually the disruptive ones, testing the adult. Ashley led the group in contesting the researcher. The day the interviews were shifted to the gym Ashley wanted to play, "Duck, Duck, Goose." When the researcher refused this request, Ashley said that the researcher was unfair and commented, "If I was saying it about someone else, you would agree with me, wouldn't you?" The "it" to which Ashley referred was her possible complaint about the researcher's refusal to meet their request to play. She assumed that, like most authorities, the researcher would see the mote in other people's eyes, but not her own. Calculated to make the researcher feel herself as unjust as all adults, the remark was clever and demonstrated that Ashley had the skills of a politician if not an interest in the topic.

The agreement among the children about what they thought about politics, the media, justice and fairness, in school and out, was striking. They seemed to have internalized an opposition to smoking, drugs and unhealthy behaviors generally. The test of this learning, however, will come in subsequent years when they enter middle and secondary schools.

There did not seem to be differences in opinions based on socioeconomic factors or gender. The differences between the boys and girls were not in their views, but in their attitudes. The girls were also more concrete in their thinking. There was a consistency in the sixth graders' views about the treatment of bad people, whether they were criminals or unruly and unwilling students. There was also a sense that these special needs children could learn if they tried and that poor people could get jobs if they also tried. Underneath their generally liberal views was a core of conservatism that judged individuals harshly, while professing humanitarian respect for all. The two strands of school and national politics seem to come together in the children's sense of powerlessness in school and their apathy about politics, particularly on the part of the girls.

The absurdities inherent in presidential campaigns seemed epitomized by the announcement in April 2000 that Mattel was entering a Barbie for President doll into the fray. Supported by organizations such as The White House Project and Girls Incorporated, the new Barbie was supposed to inspire young women to consider politics as a career goal. Interviews with girls on National Public Radio and in press stories suggested that young women recognized a publicity stunt when they saw it.

However, another project was launched called Kids Voting.[2] With its own web site, this was an attempt to include children in politics by having them consider the issues that affected children. Picked up by schools in the fall, this campaign involved children in mock elections and in discussions of various political topics.

Theoretically, public schools were founded, not only to provide children with basic skills and knowledge, but also to teach them how to become good citizens. Democracy, according to Thomas Jefferson, could not survive without an educated citizenry. Currently, schools are joined, perhaps even surpassed, in this responsibility by the media. In a small, rural state like Vermont, the media, including the Internet, provide access to a wider world than the children experience directly. Following up on the 1996 study, the goal was to see if anything had changed in four years in children's ideas about the electoral process.

The same sixth-grade teacher, who had cooperated the last time, selected students who were similar in background to those she had chosen before. In addition, questionnaires were sent to the sixth grade classrooms in the area to set the responses of the informants into a larger context. The Kids Forum[3] web page was also checked regularly. Unfortunately, the web page that Mattel had for children to share their election concerns with Barbie was discontinued before the fall election.

Besides the interviews, the survey responses were from five schools, with nine classes represented. There were nineteen fifth-graders and one hundred forty-three sixth-graders for a total of one hundred sixty-two children, eighty-six males and seventy-six females. Most of the respondents were eleven and twelve years old.

The basic questions in the interviews were the same as those four years earlier. Naturally, the follow-up questions varied in response to the children's ideas. For the survey, ten questions that explored knowledge and attitudes about the presidency were included. There was also a question about the Barbie for President doll. The questionnaires were distributed a month before the election.

Groups are unique in that their dynamics are specific to the individuals and the situations. Some of the differences between the children interviewed in 1996 and those interviewed in 2000 were a function of their individual personalities. However, there were some changes that might indicate shifts in the social experiences of these latter children in contrast to the earlier group. The first impression that was most striking was the difference in the girls. In both groups, the boys were articulate and generally interested in discussing a range of political issues. Four years earlier, there was one girl who contributed in a lively manner to discussions, often transforming social issues into personal ones. The other three girls were generally quiet.

This time there were four eloquent girls seriously engaged in sharing their opinions. The girls were also more consistent in their political opinions, elaborating on them, but rarely changing their positions. Although the children's bent was generally liberal, as it was with the children four years earlier, the boys drifted to more conservative positions on some issues. All of them were more knowledgeable about politics than the previous group. A boy and a girl now held the steadying role of thoughtful ballast shared by two boys in the previous set of interviews. The sessions also stayed focused on the topics raised. Last time, the students had wanted to talk about school issues more than national and state politics. Although questions from the Kids Forum[4] about issues relevant to students such as dress codes, class size and teacher responsibility were used, the students' thoughtful responses did not reflect the same discontent with authority that had characterized the previous group. These children seemed at ease with their school, able to discuss their experiences with equanimity

Smoking and drugs were a major concern with the first group. When asked about what were the important issues in the school, the current students cited how people treat each other and the physical condition of the school. One of the students' objections to George Bush was that they felt that he wanted to take money from the public schools and give it to private schools.

The question about Barbie for President led, as it was supposed to, to questions about women and politics. Barbie, herself, was pretty much dismissed in the interviews and in the surveys. If Mattel was looking for positive publicity, their efforts were not successful with this group of children. On the surveys, twenty-four of the girls thought that it led to the possibility of a positive role model for girls, while thirty-four thought the idea was a terrible one and seventeen were not even aware of the doll.

The response from the boys was even stronger. Forty-eight thought the doll was a bad idea, sixteen thought it was all right, sixteen were not aware of it and three boys noted that the question was an immature one. As one girl noted, "I think that the Barbie for President doll isn't meant to do anything but to make the company who made it more money."

Not surprisingly, the observations about women in politics were richer in the discussions than on the surveys since there was only one question on the survey to which the children responded. The question was "Why do you think we have never had a woman president?" There was a gender difference in the reaction between the boys and the girls on the survey. More boys tended to think women had not wanted to be president than did girls, twenty-seven to six. Forty-one girls wrote that people did not think women were good enough while thirty-three boys indicated that as the reason. A typical response from one of the boys was, "People can be prejudiced and not feel women can do the job."

In responding directly to the question of why we have never had a woman president, the interviewed students responded that people were afraid of change or didn't think women were capable. They also referred to women's history of not having the vote. One boy liked to call for votes on particular questions. When he did this time, all eight of the students voted in support of the idea of a woman president. This was consistent with the view of the students in 1996.

The issue of women in politics was one that kept appearing in the context of different discussions. For example, although they praised Vice President Gore for appointing a Jewish running mate, they faulted him for not selecting a woman. They did not apply this same standard to Governor Bush. Some of their reasons had to do with how they perceived Bush's personality. "He's too self-centered," but others had to do with their awareness of Bush's and the Republican's stance on abortion, an issue on which the children had various views. The boys wavered in their opinions on this whereas the girls were steadfast in their belief in a woman's right to choose.

Four years ago the school's involvement in teaching children about the election had been minimal, but this time the children were assigned to watch the debates and there was a steady influx of news articles, culminating with the involvement of all the children working on the Kids Voting[5] project. Meeting with them on Election Day had to be fit in between their responsibilities checking off names and helping other students vote. The children thought a great deal about what was the best way to be informed about the elections. In agreement with the children on the survey, the students did not like the political advertisements on television. In the surveys fifty-six boys disliked them, while only twenty-four thought they had value and six were neutral in their assessment of them. Thirty-nine of the girls disliked them, twenty were neutral and seventeen thought they had value. All of the children in the interviews objected to negative ads. There was general agreement that if you don't have anything nice to say, you shouldn't say anything at all. The children were even skeptical of the non-attack ads. As one of them said, "I think some commercials might lie a little bit. I don't think Ruth Dwyer (the Republican candidate for governor) spent all that time helping that kid on the horse."

Although they, like the students four years earlier, found much of the television coverage boring, these students were more focused because they had specific assignments while they were watching the debates. Initially, all eight students supported Vice President Gore, primarily because they did not like Governor Bush's television persona. By Election Day some of them had shifted their allegiance. When asked on that day if they were excited, one boy said, "I'm not really up on my feet jumping for joy because in some ways I don't like either of them."

Besides the inclusion of the surveys, there were some other aspects of this study that made it unique when contrasted with the one conducted four years earlier. Obviously, the contested election made for a different final day interview. The other important factor was that the Vermont State election was hotly contested because of the issue of civil unions. The previous spring, under order from the Vermont Supreme Court, the Vermont legislature had passed a bill providing same sex couples all the rights and benefits of married couples. The legislature carefully distinguished these unions from traditional marriages. Nonetheless, there were signs all over the state to Take Back Vermont. The children were very aware of this issue and addressed it early in the interviews.

When asked what was the most important issue in Vermont, the children first agreed on taxes. Then one student said, "Wait a minute. The law that promotes gays to get married. I think there are people against it." None of the children saw anything wrong with the idea of civil unions. One girl turned to the girl sitting next to her and putting her hand on her arm said, "If she was gay, I would still like her. She would still be my friend." This attitude about gays was generally consistent throughout the interviews. However, at one point a boy said, "The Lord. In His eyes He sees people as a man and a woman. Not a man and a man. Not a woman and a woman. A man and a woman." To which, a girl asked, "What if people can't help themselves? What if it's just that their bodies feel different?" The children considered this silently.

Discussions about gays were often mingled with ideas about blacks. One week the children spoke earnestly about how to explain differences among people to younger children. Their first example was of a boy who dressed like a girl. In the midst of this discussion, a girl chimed in with her experience about when she was younger and had loudly pointed out a brown person. Her mother slapped her and she learned not to do it again. Advising what to do with younger children, one boy said, "Tell them they are not different, they just look different. They just have different color skin." Another boy agreed, "They are like us. They bleed the same color as us."

The week after the election, one boy said about the re-elected Governor, "He should take Vermont back to the way it used to be." At that, another child replied, "Used to be people going around killing people. No homos." When I asked if they had changed their minds about civil unions, they agreed they had not. However, one boy said, "It has made us the laughing stock of United States." When asked why, he answered, "We are the only state. The first schools that let blacks in were like that." Once again this led to talk discussing the few blacks in their school and how it was dumb if people weren't comfortable in a class with people of a different color.

Another theme that kept emerging in the children's consideration of the presidency and the election was President's Clinton's affair with Monica Lewinsky. Four years earlier, Clinton had been the children's choice for president. This group of children, however, continuously referred to his lying about his relationship with Lewinsky. "I think he should not have been kicked out of office, but he should have paid a penalty for lying to the country." When asked what was the worst thing a president could do, the children agreed that lying under oath was. This concern with lying was also evident in the children's reactions to the information about Governor Bush's drunk driving. They thought his reason for not revealing this information was "lame." He was compared to Clinton. One student observed that, "If he wants to keep it from his daughters, that's pretty bad, because then he would keep more stuff from them."

In the last interview, when discussing the results of the contested election, the children thought nothing much was going to change except, "They'll all end up cheating on their wives anyway." This marital cheating became fused with electoral cheating in the children's discouraged assessment of the election results.

When asked if the election was fair the children did not think so. "Lots of people might think if they have a revote, Gore cheated. Lots of people might think Bush cheated if they don't have a revote." This and their general assumption that politicians do not keep their promises left a much more dispirited group of children at the end of this election as compared to the children four years previously. Then it was noted that they saw the political process as generally fair and politicians as working to solve the country's problems. This clearly contrasted with the sentiment the current students expressed. "Most of the time they really don't do what they say they are going to do. . ." This was much closer to the views expressed by children in the non-election year of 1995.

"They might try to do it like they try to do it, but sometimes they can't do it. There's too much people saying no to it or something." Their advice to whomever was going to be president. "Don't make promises you can't keep."

This air of disillusionment was also present in the children's comments about people who did not vote. They felt that either people didn't care or didn't have a chance to vote. One boy stated, "I know a lady who doesn't vote. She used to be my neighbor. She doesn't vote because they say your vote counts and it really doesn't." When challenged that this election would seem to disprove that, he and some other children conceded that this election was different. Others were still not convinced that votes counted.

What makes this response particularly interesting was that the children on the survey given before the election, asked what they thought about people who didn't vote, were generally quite tolerant of people who didn't vote. Once again, there were differences between the boys and girls. Forty-one girls thought it was all right if people didn't vote. Only twenty-eight were upset by the idea that they didn't, while five had no opinion.

Thirty-two of the boys thought not voting was acceptable as contrasted with forty-nine that did not approve, with five not commenting. A typical response from both boys and girls was expressed by this girl, "I don't think that much about people who don't vote because if they do or don't want to vote it is their decision, not ours." Given the large number of non-voters in our country, this attitude seems prevalent and likely to continue unless programs like Kids Vote lead to a greater sense of civic responsibility in our population.

There are a number of lessons that can be learned from this investigation. The first is the striking difference between the knowledge and behavior of the girls from the last election to this. Four years ago the girls often complained that they were just kids and too young to be engaged in thinking about politics. They often expressed themselves through personal anecdotes rather than abstract reasoning. This was not at all the response of this year's group of four girls. When asked how they decided whom to vote for during Kids Vote, there was a range of responses but the most definitive one was from a girl. "The way I've come up with whom I'd vote for is I've read about the candidates, seen the candidates on tv, heard about them on the radio. Then all the stuff I know. I'm sure 100 percent of it is not true, but some of it's probably true. I like most of the ideas from the people I chose."

When the issue of a dress code or school uniforms was discussed, the girls were firm that uniforms or not, girls would not wear dresses or skirts to school. One of their reasons was annoyance with boys lifting skirts and the other was the ease and comfort of pants. The girls' consistency of views did not seem rigid because they always had valid explanations for their positions. The boys seemed more liable to repeat slogans and catch phrases, such as "We're the laughing stock."

Although the children four years ago also expressed acceptance of people of color, developmentally and behaviorally disabled children, who were a part of Vermont's inclusion program, upset and angered them. Not only was there no mention of this program this year, but the children's grappling with the issues presented by Vermont's Civil Unions Bill showed them to be capable of seeing many sides of a complex situation.

What is perhaps a more cautionary lesson is the disillusionment of the children with their political leaders. Whereas children four years ago had faith in the democratic process, two major events have shaken these children's beliefs. President Clinton's mendacity not only made him a recurring negative example of a politician, but also tainted the children's views of all politicians. Coupled with the negative stance of the media, particularly attack ads on television,

Clinton's behavior made them distrustful of the country's leadership. The contested election confirmed their distrust of the system. When interviewed the week after the election much of the situation had not yet been played out. It was clear that the children's confidence in the system had not been restored. Through programs such as Kids Vote, schools have taken a proactive stance in educating children about our system of government. This can not be addressed only once every four years. The complexities of our society with which children are confronted through the media challenge their cognitive and social maturity. They need ongoing assistance in understanding and evaluating their world. This became clear in the interviews and surveys conducted in 2004.

As in the 2000 election, surveys were given to the entire sixth grade public school classes in the district supplementing the interviews. There were six schools with a total of two hundred children, divided into one hundred boys and one hundred girls. The same questionnaire was used except that the question about the Barbie for President doll was replaced with one that asked what the children thought was the best way for kids to learn about politics.

Besides the group interviews, children from another school were also interviewed in the context of a college class. The ongoing group interviews were conducted in the original school. However, there was a new teacher who was also most cooperative in selecting the children. In the interviews, this time the boys clearly dominated the conversations. This contrasted with the situation in the 2000 election study, where the interviewed girls were outspoken. However, it was consistent with how the girls functioned in the 1996 interviews. Girls would respond to direct questioning but only rarely volunteered information or opinions.

On the surveys, however, the girls' answers were far more extensive than the boys,' indicating, perhaps, a greater ease on the boys' parts with expressing themselves orally. A clue to the girls' stance may be suggested by the response that a sixth-grade girl in the college class interviews gave to the question of why we have never had a woman president. "She would have to stand up in front of all those people and make speeches. She would be nervous." A follow-up interview with the group in May 2005 to ask them about how they felt about the election six months later found the girls more outspoken than they had been in the fall, seemingly readier than the boys, at least socially, for middle school.

The issue of why we have never had a woman president is one that indicated some of the changes over time in children's understanding and attitudes. In the past this question had usually elicited a response that focused on history and on people's general inability to accept change with assurances on the part of both males and females that a woman president would be desirable. In the current surveys, this was not the case. Answers that might be considered to place the blame on women for this lack were offered by fifty-seven of the boys. One eleven year old boy answered the question with, "because they are not as smart as us boys." Responses that reflected male prejudice against women were sixteen in number and history was cited in eleven cases. (Figures do not always add up to one hundred because some children did not answer some questions or indicated that they did not know the answers) Only five boys thought that women were capable of running for office and winning an election. A lone voice suggested that not only was the current situation a result of historic forces, but it should be changed. "Because men always run, but I personally think a black woman should be president."

The girls had somewhat different views. Only twenty-three of them saw the fault in women's insecurity or lack of trying. Fifty-four of them saw a preference for men; seven cited historical reasons. There was a much greater range of responses to this question from the girls than from the boys. For example, one girl noted, "Men are better for the job," while another wrote, "Because woman are better than men and men can't except that! [sic]" Both anger and reason were expressed. ". . . because half of the population are men and men are pigs" as well as, "I think the reason we've never had a woman president is that women don't have the desire to rule, their desire is to raise their kids right."

In the group interviews the idea that men were better at running the government was the dominant view without even the acknowledgement that this might be unfair to women, as had been expressed by some of the girls on the surveys. Indeed, women were perceived as having a special skill in raising children while men were seen to argue more effectively than women. This was in sharp contrast to the views expressed by children in 1996 and 2000 where it was felt that women should have an opportunity to become president and to take part in government.

As happens in talking with children over time, shifts do occur. Angela, who initially had to be coaxed to say anything, by the fifth meeting, was more open. When the children were discussing going to college after high school, Angela noted that she would not go because she was going to be her father's secretary. Her brothers were going to take over the business. Responding to gentle chiding from the others, she did acknowledge that she might take over the business with them as well as run for a local political office.

How do these ideas develop in children? Asking the children on the surveys what was the best way for children to learn about politics, twenty-eight of the boys indicated television, twenty-two said school, fifteen cited newspapers and books, eight referred to parents and six specified the Internet. Other responses were less than five in number and included other people, video games and cartoons. Girls' replies were similar. Thirty-four responses noted school as a source, while thirty-one cited television and thirteen reported learning from other people. Newspapers and books were tied with parents at eleven and the Internet received eight mentions.

Whether the low reference to parents suggests a shift in the source of knowledge for children or only a lack of recognition on the part of the children of how central parents are to their political ideas may be illuminated by the interviews. When asked if the children talked about politics with their parents, one boy noted that on Sundays, "when we are all together at dinner" was when such conversations occurred. However, there were indications in the course of the interviews that there was much more of an influence than the children articulated. In talking about video games, the boys reported how their fathers told them that war was not at all like the games. "Nobody is safe. Everyone is scared. War is completely different than those games. There is never that one chance."

The war dominated all of the discussions as well as the surveys. When asked what was the most important issue that we had in the United States, seventy-one of the boys and sixty-one of the girls cited the war and terrorism. The rest of the responses were scattered. When asked the most important issue for children, the children responded education with health care a close second.

An indication of how children used their media knowledge to understand political situations was demonstrated by Phillip's analysis.

> We should have stayed in Afghanistan and hunted them (the terrorists) out. When I play a game of medieval total war, every time that I was at war with a big country in it, I would never try to fight other armies that were potential threats. I would defeat the army I was dealing with first before dealing with other ones, which Bush obviously didn't do. He was too eager to jump into Iraq. Maybe because of his father.

Phillip then went on to explain that he also read a lot of books that had a lot of politics in them. He describe a science fiction book that he and another one of the boys had read that told him a great deal about politics and war. The other children agreed that in the game *Age of Empires*, for example, you had to have enough food, gold and wood. "It's got to be completely balanced. If your economy is too low and military too high, you are just going to die."

Besides video games, the children learned from the Internet. Most of these children and those who came to my class had computers and all had access to computers either in school or at home. When asked if they visited specific sites designed for children, Phillip replied that he just "googled" a topic in which he was interested.

The children also thought that the History Channel was cool. When asked about their television preferences, the children who came to the college class replied the Cartoon Network, The Disney Channel, Sports, never specifying a particular program but only a location of similar programs.

replied the Cartoon Network, The Disney Channel, Sports, never specifying a particular program but only a location of similar programs.

Our other discussions of the media focused on advertisements and the debates. From the surveys the views on political advertisements were evenly divided between seeing them as an annoyance or as a positive source of information with the boys and girls in agreement on their assessments. The children objected to negative commercials. They wanted ads that were informative.

Unlike during the previous elections, the children attended to the debates more seriously and were able to articulate their views about the candidates. Their focus was on personality and process rather than on content, much like the students in Buckingham's interviews. How did the candidates handle themselves? How did they relate to each other? What was the object on President Bush's back in the second debate? Vice President Cheney came in for criticism, not only for his performance on camera, but for his previous behavior. Children do not approve of public figures swearing. The children were not, however, particularly mindful that his target had been a Vermont senator.

Outside of the president and the governor, children had little awareness of other political figures. Even when one girl was disparaging the Vermont representative to Congress, she kept referring to Barney rather than Bernie (Sanders). This was another case of parental influence that was probably underestimated in the surveys. She disliked him because, "My parents said he was evil." Why? "Haven't a clue."

As noted previously, research has consistently asserted the centrality of the presidential figure in children's concept of politics. This was confirmed in both the surveys and the interviews, not only in the role assigned to the president, but also in the children's ignorance about others in the political system. Children had little idea about what the governor did or what the functions of legislators or the Supreme Court were.

Both boys and girls saw the President as a powerful figure. According to them, he either rules or runs the country. In some cases, his dominion extends to the world. He makes laws, raises and lowers taxes, helps people and runs the military. Some children mentioned his working with others, but the majority seemed to see a figure working alone to protect the country and to make all the necessary decisions. The image that emerges is more like a monarchy than a democracy.

When asked what advice they would give the President, some of the children demurred, noting that as an eleven or twelve year old, they weren't in a position to advise the President. Some, however, were very clear. Stop the war. Lower taxes on the middle class and "higher" them on the wealthy. Many were concerned that the President be honest. Lying on the part of politicians was a concern expressed in several different contexts. One eleven-year-old girl made this plea. "Please stop being against everyone The Bible said to forgive our enemies, not to get revenge on them.[sic]"

There was a range of ideas as to what was the first thing children would do if they were President. For most of the girls the emphasis was on social and domestic programs including providing jobs for people, health insurance, better education. However, for a good number of the children (sixty-one), stopping the war was the first priority. Boys also had more personal agendas than girls did such as "Try to get everyone to like me" and "say that kids get gym and recess all day." However, boys did also advocate for jobs and aid to the homeless among their social issues.

One eleven-year-old girl affirmed that the first thing she would do would be:

> cut back on wellfare. We should stop paying extra money so they can go get food and sit on their butts for hours. They don't even have to work. All they do is suck money out of tax payers they are sitting on their porch. We are out breaking our backs and erning money to feed our familys but it goes strate to wellfare from our taxes. Also I would lower gas and oil prices.[sic]

On the other hand, a twelve-year-old boy stated:

> I would donate 5,000 to the homeless shelters across the world and bring are troops home and the making of schools in iraq, africa, or any other places that don't have any schools in the district of the state.[sic]

Some of the children on the surveys suggested that they would lower the voting age so that children would be more involved and so that children's issues such as child abuse would be addressed. In discussing this with the interview group, there were a variety of views expressed. Some thought that eighteen was a good age because then people were old enough to understand the issues. Others suggested fourteen or sixteen as possible voting ages. Objections to the younger ages were raised because the children were not old enough to understand politics.

To the question of whether all adults understood politics, the response was a resounding negative. We then explored what would be necessary to help children understand politics. The children suggested a history class to be taken the last year of high school or the first year of college. Everyone should have to take it, but it should be interesting. Not a class where someone just got up and spoke, but a group such as we were or even better, a class in which there were projects. Conrad shared information about a class that his father had taken where there were fifty people in the class. Everyone was divided into groups and each group became a country that had to negotiate with other countries. Cries of "cool" and "awesome" greeted this example. In many ways the proposal sounded like a live video game that engaged the players interactively.

Discussion of the issues these countries would face led to thinking about what makes a good citizen of a country. One girl, Mira, whose name and color suggested that she was Pakistani, said that, "They shouldn't judge people by their culture or their skin color." The children concurred. She then went on to talk about her father, "My Dad, he was not born in this country. I was. When he was working in a casino, some people would say to him, 'Go back to your own country.'"

Janet chimed in with her own experience of being discriminated against. As a Mormon, she and her family went to a summer program where Baptists boycotted them with signs proclaiming, "God can't take away all your sins." They responded by singing hymns, but it hurt that their religion was not respected.

Mira turned to her friend, "The first time we saw each other, we didn't think much of each other. Then we got to be friends." The children acknowledged this and tried to think how to help new children in class. "Don't give them that group stare," Philip suggested.

Mira continued, "My Dad owns a motel and some people just go away right after they look at my dad or my mom. So we don't get as much as other people might. It affects business, relationships. People should care more. They shouldn't just judge. There is nothing really different."

This episode illustrated the multicultural society in which these children are growing up. On a personal level they responded to Mira with friendship and acceptance. There was a kindness and generosity in the children's face to face exchanges that was missing at times in the surveys. This was most evident in some statements about welfare recipients. Gay marriage was not generally an issue. Four years ago, because of the Civil Unions legislation in Vermont there was extensive discussion about homosexuality among the children interviewed while it was barely mentioned this time. I asked them only because of President Bush's proposed amendment to the Constitution. The interviewed children took the stance, "Whatever people decide to do they should be able to do, no matter how strange it may seem to be."

Issues that were significant four and eight years ago such as drugs, smoking and alcohol, although mentioned, were minimized. The war and terrorism shifted the children's emphasis to more global issues involving the environment and the lack of allies the United States had. In talking about their memories of 9/11, the children, who were then in third grade, remembered their confusion about the event. One boy's stepmother was an airline stewardess and had gone to New York to work that morning. He was relieved when she called him from Philadelphia to assure him she was all right.

Our last session was the day after the election. Some of the group were disappointed with the outcome. In their Kids Vote election, Kerry had won. Just as this was the first time that the election on Nickelodeon[6] had not predicted the outcome, so these children found it difficult to accept the results. They made fun of President Bush having said after he voted that he was going to spend quality time with his wife. As in the last election, President Bush's personality was not one that the children found appealing.

When asked what was going to change, the children felt that nothing would, that President Bush wanted to keep on going as he was. They thought he would reinstate the draft and lower taxes. They were scornful of people who didn't vote unlike the children on the survey, who were again evenly divided, arguing that although people should vote, they have the right to chose. As in 2000, the survey questions were answered before the election. In both cases those who sympathized with the non-voters were not aware what an impact they would have on the outcome.

One boy noted that we were turning into an evil country because Bush had started the war. As a group they once again reiterated their insistence that we should have finished in Afghanistan before going into Iraq. Osama Bin Laden, one girl claimed, had better health care than we did and our taxes were paying for it. Her teacher had told her so. He was eating well at our expense. She had confused Saddam Hussein with Bin Laden, but her sense of justice was still outraged whoever the prisoner might be.

This led to a discussion of the death penalty. The children expressed indignation that the appeal process took so long. "We should kill prisoners right away rather than pay for their teeth and their food." One boy suggested that we torture the prisoners first and then kill them.

When asked if the leaders of all countries should be treated the same way, Philip, always the most reasonable of the group, noted that if leaders had been striving for peace there should be some leniency. After struggling with this concept for a while, the group agreed that all nation heads should be treated the same way after a war.

The children's facility with slogans arose when they described themselves, first as the children of tomorrow and then as the adults of tomorrow. This led into the question of what they would want in a President when they were adults. There was general agreement that it should be a person who was honest, loyal and dedicated to achieving a peaceful world. Honesty was the trait most often stressed.

This led to a discussion of the types of policies that a president or a governor should enact. The children were most concerned that the governor improve the schools with new desks, books and computers. Conrad, bright and eager as usual, proposed the following policy.

> The State of Vermont should like really reduce taxes and make it so you only have to pay for your child instead of always having to pay for somebody else's child cause say there's somebody that everybody who goes to school if they do have enough money to pay for themselves and just themselves, I don't think they should have to squeeze every last penny out of their pocket.[sic]

When asked, "Suppose somebody can't pay?"
"Then they don't need to go to school."
This led to the question of what someone would do to be a good citizen of the community. Pick up litter, recycle, and don't smoke in front of kids, were the answers offered. They all agreed that everyone should have health care, but declined to raise taxes to pay for it.

This sense of the individual was also demonstrated in the children's discussion about the draft. Not only were they strongly opposed to the draft, but they also felt that the soldiers who had refused to go on a convoy mission in Iraq were right in their refusal. "We are supposed to be free and all. We shouldn't be forced to go to war if someone doesn't want to."

Unlike other countries where the political socialization of children may be more tightly controlled, in the United States there are myriad conflicting influences on children, not to mention the experiences they have in complex, changing communities. Therefore, it is probably not surprising that the children hold many contradictory ideas. On the one hand, they are open, accepting and caring and on the other, worried and begrudging. The economic situation is uncertain and the war and terrorism are a constant threat to them that they can barely control. Many children on the surveys talked about the war indirectly when they thought the most important issue for kids was the absence of family members who were soldiers.

The media also tells these children to be skeptical, if not distrustful of their leaders. The children noted how movies, except for *Air Force One*, made Presidents look like fools and cowards. Their cinematic image of this powerful figure was him cowering under a desk when being threatened by an assassin. Beyond this, they were continuously troubled by the idea of the unreliability of their leaders. The dramatic confrontation between forces of good and evil that the media highlights make it difficult for them not to see villains. Often, they were the same people, the poor and hungry in the world that they wanted to feed and the welfare cheats who "sat on their butts"; the president who could help the world, but also start an unnecessary war.

The children picked up catch phrases from the rhetoric they heard from politicians. They understood that as citizens they were free to choose, as everyone was, but not necessarily to serve. Certainly, they had incorporated the idea that taxes were an anathema. Their responsibility to their fellow citizens extended to keeping the streets clean.

Yet, these were thoughtful children. Many of their answers were compassionate; their capacity for thinking not sufficiently challenged by the media, or even by the schools as they are currently evolving. If kids could vote, would they do any better than their parents in the media saturated world?

We have seen how events shape the lives of citizens, even those who are as yet too young to vote. Homosexuality that was such an issue four years ago was barely addressed this time. Currently, the war shapes their thinking and absorbs their energies, while their parents' anxieties about the economy also haunt them.

At one point the children were complaining about the No Child Left Behind Act and incessant testing. In another example of their use of instant phrases, they declared, "They are taking our childhood away from us." Thinking of how they would improve schools, they advocated a three-day weekend to compensate for all the homework they had. Deconstructing the curriculum, they threw it all out, except for math. They needed math and reading; they would need that. And spelling, yes. Slowly they reconstructed the entire curriculum, but on their terms, not boring, not "with the same stuff over and over." More like the history course they had designed to prepare themselves to vote.

Perhaps, this is one of the answers to the complexity of children learning to vote. Buckingham may be right that children, like all citizens, need to have some power in shaping their own education. They can use the media, including books, television, movies, and video games, without relinquishing the power to ask questions about what it means to live in a democracy where everyone is not yet equal and where people still make judgements based on culture, skin color and religion.

Some people have suggested that low voter turnout is the rational response to a system in which there is only the illusion of power. Once again we are confronted with the question about the amount of influence an individual vote every four years has when contrasted with the power of those who serve on boards of corporations and local governments and agencies. Or of those who contribute heavily to a political campaign. As one twelve-year-old boy responded to the question about people who did not vote. "They're cool not wasting their time voting for someone that takes all their money." Does the focus on the presidential elections give children and citizens the wrong ideas about democracy? Does it seem like just another reality show? Much has been made of the difference in voter participation for *American Idol* as contrasted with voter turnout in presidential elections.

In a follow-up interview with this group in May, the children reiterated some of the same points. All but one of them felt that President Bush was doing a bad job and that he was not a responsible leader. The No Child Left Behind legislation continued to be a contentious issue with the students. When some of the children suggested impeaching Bush and were asked on what grounds they would do so, most of them cited No Child Left Behind. As one girl said, "You don't learn what we actually need. We just learn what's on the test."

The war in Iraq, and the nature of Bush's military service during the Vietnam war continued to upset them. Even the one student who said she thought it was good that Bush had been elected did not have much that was good to say about him and his policies. They weren't much impressed with Congress either.

The increasing disillusionment of children with the political process shown in these ten years is a trend that should be watched carefully. These are not children whom the army will find easy to recruit. Even in 1996 between the two Gulf wars, there was a negative feeling about war. That feeling was not transformed once the country was at war. Just as people had the right not to vote, they had the right to decide that they would not escort a convoy if it was dangerous. The children's video game play seems to have made them less rather then more eager for war. Although distrustful of the media, they were influenced by its stories, caught up in the fear of continuous threats, while theoretically accepting people of different races and sexual orientation.

Looking at the three elections we might note certain trends intensifying. Although during all of the election cycles, the children valued honesty, they did not seem to expect it from the country's leaders. If lying about a sexual indiscretion was unforgivable to children so too were the mistakes made in the Iraq war from misinformation about the weapons of mass destruction to the lack of resolution of the war against Osama Bin Laden.

Notes

1. Carol Gilligan, Nona P. Lyons and Trudy J. Hanmer, eds., *Making Connections: The Relational Worlds of Adolescent Girls at Emma Willard School* (Cambridge, Mass: Harvard University Press, 1990) and Lyn Mikel Brown and Carol Gilligan, *Meeting at the Crossroads: Women's Psychology and Girls; Development* (Cambridge, Mass: Harvard University Press, 1992).

2. Kids Voting <http://www.kidsvotingusa.org/>

3. Kids Forum <http://www.topix.net/forum/family/kids/>

4. Kids Forum

5. Kids Voting

6. Nickelodeon <http://www.nick.com/>

Chapter Four

Politics and the Media in a Non-Election Year

In interviewing children in a non-election year there was more focus on the media than in the previous interviews and surveys. Politics and the nature of democracy were also discussed often through an examination of the media. Again there were eight children, four boys and four girls. They were from two different sixth grade classrooms in the same school; two boys and two girls from each class. The meeting space was one of the best available for the interviews; a music room at the end of a hall was quiet and secluded from the usual school traffic. The interviews were conducted over seven weeks in fall 2005 and two additional weeks in the winter, 2006. The surveys, besides including all the previous schools, added the two urban schools and one suburban school as noted earlier.

There were two hundred eighteen survey responses, forty-one from the urban population, forty-one from the suburban group and one hundred and thirty-six from the rural. The total number of females was one hundred and one and for males it was one hundred seventeen. Although a good number of urban schools were contacted in the nearby urban area in New York State and in a larger metropolitan area in New England, there were not as many responses as there were in the rural schools where the research had been going on for many years.

Some of the same questions that had been asked in previous interviews and surveys were reiterated. Questions such as *What is the most important problem in the United States today? What is the most important problem that affects children? What is the first thing you would do if you were in the government? Why haven't we had a woman president?*

In addition, they were asked, *What is democracy? How did you learn about it? How would you teach someone about it?* as well as *Who are the most important people in a democracy?*

Added to those questions was a chart about how students used their free time. A list of options such as playing outside with friends, reading, playing video games watching television, listening to music, reading comic books, working on a hobby, using the computer, and instant messaging were listed. The ratings were "not much," "sometimes," "a lot." Although these are subjective categories, the children took them seriously as indicated by some children writing in under the "not much" category, "never" or other qualifiers. They were then asked for their favorite television programs, video or computer games, books or comic books, web sites and after each of these, what they learned from them. Finally, they were asked what they wanted to learn in school.

In terms of how they spent their free time, the children interviewed and those surveyed were similar in their responses. These percentages do not show a ranking between the different activities, but how much the children engage in each activity. Among urban, suburban and rural males estimating whether they played outside with friends not much, sometimes and a lot, 58 percent reported a lot. Thirty-one percent sometimes and 11 percent not much. The girls were not far behind with 54 percent of them saying that they also played outside with friends a lot. The differences in video game playing between boys and girls were what might be expected. Forty-one percent of the boys reported playing a lot while only 16 percent of the girls did. Of the boys, 18 percent said they read a lot, compared to 46 percent who read sometimes and 36 percent who read not much, while with girls the comparable figures were 26 percent, a lot, 48 percent sometimes and 26 percent not much. The figures on watching television were much closer. For males, 39 percent reported watching a lot, 40 percent sometimes, and 21 percent not much. For females, the figures were 39 percent a lot, 43 percent sometimes and 18 percent not much.

Most extreme were the figures for reading comic books. Six percent of the boys said they read them a lot, 11 percent sometimes and 83 percent not much. The girls' report of their reading indicated that 5 percent read them a lot, 8 percent sometimes and 87 percent not much. The similarities in the boys and girls comic book reading is somewhat surprising, given the conventional wisdom that, as with video games, comic books are more popular with boys than girls. Since studies show that activities are usually displaced by similar activities, television viewing and video games probably take precedence over comic books. With the recent revival of interest in comic books via the graphic novel, it is somewhat surprising to see so little interest in them. This may have something to do with the age level of the informants as well as the impact of other media. Comic books and graphic novels are expensive relative to television. Although video games are expensive, they involve many hours of play and may be played by more than one member of a family. Also many of the children play the games on their computers. For the rural population comic books may also not be as accessible. Even though many book store chains are now stocking graphic novels and Manga, those chains are not in the local communities.

Although the questionnaires asked about books, comic books, television programs, video and computer games as well as web sites, the interviews focused primarily on television, with some attention to video games and web sites.

The children used the media to criticize the media. In the interviews, one boy cited the Adam Sandler *Mr. Deeds* movie to make the point that newscasters can distort the news by editing. The children also use the media to discuss issues outside the media that they perhaps need to discuss with adults. Although it may be disconcerting to an adult for an eleven-year old girl to report that *Law and Order: Special Victims Unit* is her favorite television show, children might be able to clarify some of their concerns if they could discuss such programs with adults.

For each interview session there was a list of questions to start the discussions although at times not all the questions were answered because follow-up questions to the children's responses would take the conversation into different areas. The children in the interviews were thoughtful and cooperative although, as in the other interviews, the boys dominated the discussions. Even in the 2000 interviews where all the girls participated more fully than in any other group, the boys were the major contributors in terms of frequency and extensiveness of their comments. In the spring session of the 2004 group, the girls were more active than they had been in the fall, but still did not equal the boys with one girl maintaining her limited role. In the 2005-2006 interviews all the boys were active, with two of the girls holding their own, one contributing occasionally and one girl, although attentive, primarily silent. Only in the first and last few sessions, would she give one word or "I don't know" answers when asked directly for her views.

One of the reasons for the surveys was to see if the children interviewed were more or less consistent with the feelings among a larger group of sixth-graders. This turned out generally to be the case. The interviews however allowed for greater detail and for a closer view of the way in which the children came to their conclusions. For example, when both the children on the surveys and in the interviews were asked what was the most important problem in the United States today, the war and Katrina were the first and most frequently mentioned followed by the price of gas.

The President was also seen as a problem both in the interviews and on the surveys. Over five years of interviews and surveys, the President as an individual was not perceived as an appealing figure, even though the President as an office was most frequently cited as the most important person in a democracy. Although the surveys were not specific in the reasons for the disapproval of this particular President, the interviews were. Criticisms were recurrent and focused on his military record and his general trustworthiness. There was indignation that he would send soldiers to war when he had never gone himself. When questioned as to what they would ask President Bush if they could, the answers included

"Why did you make our country horrible?"
"Why did you make people hate us?"
"Why did we go to war?"
To this last question one of the boys responded, "We went for oil."
A recurring theme that politicians, along with newscasters, were dishonest surfaced over and over again throughout the interviews. Children have learned

to be suspicious of what politicians and people in the media tell them. Again, this is a familiar refrain. None of the interviewed children except Mary wanted to go into politics. Mary wanted to be President, but declined to discuss what she would do if she were President. Children on the surveys, questioned as to what they would do if they were in the government, ranged in their answers from helping the homeless and the poor to lowering gas prices. However, the majority said that they would stop the war.

Both the survey and interview children demonstrated a mixture of idealism and cynicism that seemed to emerge from their developmental stage where fairness is an issue and a moral sense is being refined. The cynicism, to some degree, grows from the media world in which they live. For example, the interview children's responses to commercials reflected distrust of the media. Even though they could sing the commercials and were particularly eager to do so, they recognized that they were meant to sell products that individuals might not need.

"It's not really good because kids will go to their parents and ask them for money and the parents will say no and they will put up a big fuss about it."

"I think commercials are very distracting because sometimes you are going to commercials and like you ask, "What was I just watching?" You sit there and I forget and then it comes on and you say, 'Oh yeah.'"

". . .but I think it is just so weird the impact of so many different ads and like in a two minute period like buy a blender, buy a car, buy a toothbrush, buy a ripping. . . ."

Besides the commercials, some of the programs suggest dubious morality. As one boy noted, *Law and Order* teaches you how to lie. On news programs, the children see politicians accusing each other of telling lies.

When asked about where they got their news, the children said the newspaper and television. However, newscasters were consistently perceived to be among those who would lie in order to "make a quick buck." The girls thought that television was better than a teacher because television provided pictures. Roy said, "I think teachers are better than newscasters. A teacher really gives you details about certain things he's teaching you and the newscasters give you a short little thing about it and then move on to something else."

Joe added, "I think teachers are better than newscasters because most of the time newscasters lie to you about things."

In contrast to politicians and newscasters, teachers were seen as reliable and trustworthy. They were most often cited as the source of the children's knowledge of democracy. Democracy is a part of the fifth-grade curriculum and children both in the surveys and the interviews often indicated that. When asked what is democracy, seventeen percent of the survey children either did not answer the question or said that they did not know. Forty percent said that a democracy had to do with voting. Other answers ranged from "It's a political environment; an organized system to help solve problems" to "Having different freedoms. Some are freedom of speech and press" to "Something with the government." There were a few responses that demonstrated confusion such as "Democracy is when there is a feud between countries" or "Democracy is when someone treats someone differently because of how they look (skin color), nationality, etc."

In these survey answers, as in most of the responses to the questions, the rural children seemed more articulate and sophisticated in their understanding than the urban and suburban children. Since the urban and suburban populations were much smaller, this may have been a function of the size of the sample. There was also a consistent difference across settings between females and males in the extensiveness and clarity of their written responses. This was not as striking in the suburban sample as in the rural and urban surveys. This contrasts with the behavior of the girls in the interview situation where they did not speak as extensively as the boys did.

Discussing how democracy should be taught, the interview children had suggestions for teachers ranging from a "big course on talking to children" so that teachers would learn how to be sure children were listening and did not bore them. Joe observed, "There is a fact that teachers do not know. Children cannot pay attention to one thing for more than twelve minutes." Sarah wanted harder work in sixth grade since she was going to be a forensic scientist or cancer researcher and she wanted more knowledge.

Survey responses to the question *If you were in the government, what would be the first thing that you would do*, were consistent across all of the groups, urban, suburban, rural, male and female. They were generally serious and concerned beyond themselves. Only two rural males replied, "Let soda be in all schools" and "School four days a week." One suburban girl wrote, "Make it a rule. NO HOMEWORK." These children were the exceptions however. Fifty-two of the children said to stop the war in Iraq. Other answers focused on helping the poor and the homeless. It seemed clear from their responses to this question and to the previous questions about the problems in the country and for children that the children were affected by the impact of the hurricanes on children's lives as well as those of adults. Unlike answers in 2004, there did not seem to be overt hostility towards poor people. A few mentioned lowering taxes, but generally the role of government, as these children saw it, was to assist people.

There were perhaps three responses that might be considered generally hostile. "Kill Osama Bin Laden, Send more spies to Iraq, and World domination." The rest of the responses confronted the range of issues confronting the United States with a concern for solving problems and helping people. The children wanted to pass restrictive laws around issues that harmed people such as smoking and drugs. One suburban boy proposed, "Make fast food industries illegal but tell all workers a year in advance to find new jobs." One rural girl wanted to pass a law banning abortion and one rural male wanted a law against gay marriages. Generally, however, the children wanted to clean up the environment, lower gas prices, help fund schools and as one urban male put it, "Try to help people as much as I could."

At one point with the interview children, the conversation about what one would do in government turned to the issue of constitutional amendments, leading then to questions about last year's proposed amendments about flag burning and banning gay marriages. Roy was quick to point out that as a boy scout he had learned that the proper way to dispose of the American flag was to cut it in strips and burn it. The proposed gay marriage amendment elicited a range of responses that were similar to the views children expressed in 2000.

As they talked about gay marriage, Sarah said, "I would be very mad at someone who said only men and women can get married. . . . If two women or two guys want to get married, that's their choice."

When Joe protested that he thought that was sick, Sarah replied, "It may be gross to you, but not to them. I'm not going to do it, but I'm not going to say it's gross. It's normal to them, but not to us."

As the discussion progressed and reference was made to the television program *Will and Grace*, it was clear that attitudes were influenced by that program as well as by Vermont's Civil Union law.

The question of why we have never had a woman president was on all of the surveys over the past five years. There was a great deal of similarity in the responses between males and females, urban, suburban and rural. Although there were a few comments such as "They are girls don't know nothing." (sic) from a boy and from a girl "Some men think that woman can't do anything that man can do but we can," there were relatively few comments that saw the fault as within women. Nor did most articulate that it was men's antagonism towards women that was the culprit. The major reason given by all the surveyed groups was that it was "people" who thought that men were better suited for the job than women. This contrasted sharply with questionnaire responses just a year earlier. Whether the lack of intensity around this issue was because it was an election off year or for some other reason is difficult to know. There did not seem anything equivalent to Katrina to modify their perspectives.

Fluctuations from year to year, particularly when the informants are different is to be expected. It is the overall direction that is important. Perhaps most interestingly, the amorphous "other people" who don't think women up to the job represent the generalized other that individuals use as a contrast to themselves or as a support for their views. Just as adults and children are not concerned about the impact of the media upon themselves, but upon others, so it is other people who think those unfortunate ideas or do those unfortunate deeds.

The interview group responded to this issue of a woman president twice; early on in the interviews and at the end of the interviews when they had been asked to look at *Commander-in-Chief*, the new television program that featured a woman president. Although the children were always willing to respond to the questions about politics, they felt that they were the experts on television and video games in way that they did not feel when talking about politics.

As they discussed the woman president issue their responses were similar to those on the surveys. People, among them politicians, did not think that women were capable, although clearly they were. There was also no history of a woman president although at one point Mike thought Eleanor Roosevelt had been president. Roy suggested that if a test was given, women would have higher IQs than most of the men. Roy's evidence for this was, "Sometimes when there is tight games and like you can't get out, usually someone comes over and helps and that's usually a girl."

"Only in movies, dear," Jane commented to general laughter.

In discussing the plot of the episode, the children reviewed the problem facing the President. A man was holding the Presidential plane hostage after letting all of the people leave it. Complicating the issue was that the man was a good man with a legitimate complaint. The hijacker was a former army officer who had served the country valiantly; his wife had cancer and because his ailments had improved, their government insurance benefits were cut off. The speaker of the House was antagonistic to the president because he had wanted her to resign when she was vice president so that he could be president. The students realized that the president was being tested to demonstrate whether she would act assertively. The double vision of viewing the situation from the narrative perspective and the production aspect was evident in the children's observation that the two hostages that were released were "very important people to the show." The children are sophisticated enough viewers to know that the stars of a program will not usually be killed, no matter what danger threatens them.

This particular episode did raise the perennial issue of whether women have the courage to take the country to war, drop an atomic bomb or do whatever is necessary to defend the country. The conflict is not really between the President and the hostage taker, but between the President and the Speaker. Theoretically, the problem of how to act is intensified for a woman since the Speaker shows no qualms at all about having the man shot, and, in fact, enjoys the President's dilemma. When the president says she will talk to the man, it is clear that those around her see it as a sign of weakness. However, she makes it clear that she will not negotiate with him and that his alternative is to surrender or be shot. She does combine firmness with compassion by giving him five minutes. Not all of the episodes of this series are as metaphorically fit as this one which was randomly assigned to the students, but they were able to see the issues when given the opportunity to discuss them.

The children did not regularly watch this program or *West Wing*, being far more fascinated by mystery programs. For this group, given the amount of time they spent discussing it, *CSI* was a clear favorite. Not only did it provide Sarah with her career goal, (she was going to be either a forensic scientist or do cancer research), but it led to much speculation about the nature of crime and punishment.

Although mentioned among the survey respondents' favorites, *CSI* did not dominate them. There was a great deal of variety in the television programs that students watched. Sports and science programs were popular, as were situation comedies. When students were asked what they learned from television programs, there was a range of responses. If they watched programs like *Animal Planet*, not surprisingly the children would indicate they learned about animals. From *Law and Order*, children learn how to fight crime, from *Full House*, how to get along with family members. Some would say, "Nothing. It's entertainment," but they were not in the majority. Most of the children either reported factual information they had acquired or ways of dealing with others in conflict and other situations. Adventure programs showed them taking risks was worthy. One suburban girl, writing about the Disney Channel said, "almost everything. Like celebrities and their houses, money and life lessons."

Sarah's response to the question about detective programs that, "They make my mind work," echoed Johnson's[1] claims that contemporary media makes people smarter, because of the their technical complexity. . . Joe and Roy also were close to what Gee[2] says is the value of video games as a learning tool when Joe observed, ". . . like in video games where you have to do something to get something else, than you have to do something else to get at that and then you have to go all the way back and give the guy what he wants to get . . ."

Roy added, "It helps you figure out what you have to do to get to the next stage." This ability to think about the process by which one thinks and understands is seen by Piaget[3] as an indication of the movement towards more mature cognition. Here, the children, like some theorists, articulate learning as a function of the games they play and the television they watch.

With the interviewed children, it was possible to go into some of these lessons in further depth. In fact, the children often evoked television programs to help them think about questions that were focused away from television and on to the political situation. When talking about important laws in the country, it was clear that *CSI* and *Law and Order* provided knowledge and raised issues for the students.

Roy though that the death penalty was harsh because he had seen an episode on *CSI* where lethal injection was administered. Even though the man had been convicted of murder, Roy felt, "I mean like when you kill somebody, it's usually years ago and they're dead in a couple of seconds usually and it's good and painless. When they do it, they inject the poison and you die really slowly and hurtfully, and it really hurts."

Further discussion of this topic led to a concern about the nature of evidence and the possibility of executing an innocent person. Jane recounted an episode on *CSI*. "There's a show on *CSI* and it was like that. On the *CSI*, this lady was a forensic what not and she checked the fingerprints" (Sarah corrected her that the woman was a forensic scientist), "But she was kind of like a doctor also and she wasn't honest. People would tell her what the story was about and she just really didn't look at the fingerprints and she could just tell by her own matter. I don't think that's right. You should always just look at the fingerprints because if you don't, you might . . . . She sent ten people to jail not looking at the fingerprints."

This concern about the nature of evidence also led the children to challenge the researcher, asking how did they know she really was who she said she was. This led to an animated discussion about the nature of fact and rumor. This seemed to reflect not only the suspicion that not all the information they receive is reliable as well as the dangers of misinformation leading to wrongful convictions. Although they are not passive consumers of the media, the crime programs that the children watched caused them to focus on the significance of accurate evidence.

There were other topics that did not engage their interest. The stories that are absent from the media are as important as those that are constantly repeated.

In their analysis of the media's treatment of mothers, Douglas and Michaels[4] assert that the media does not necessarily tell audiences what to think, but what to think about. Currently, children think a great deal about crime. Part of the power of *CSI* and *Law and Order* is their pervasiveness. Not only are there several variations of the franchise running on different nights of the week, but reruns are on cable channels. Given the children's preoccupation with the nature of evidence, Douglas' and Michaels' observation that another feature of news stories is their lack of supporting evidence for their generalizations highlights the differences between news reports and the focus on evidence in crime dramas. Not only are news broadcasts shallow, but they are frequently not founded on substantive data.

Crime dramas that focus on both evidence and the moral dilemmas their protagonists face led the children think a great deal about the issues of crime and punishment. Wrongful convictions were discussed in great detail, as were the types of crimes that should lead to the death penalty. Killing in self-defense was discussed as was manslaughter and the different levels of murder about which the children seemed well informed. Still concerned about the death penalty, Roy suggested, "I think it should be limited and only used for people like serial killers and stuff, but if its like one murder or something they should probably just go to jail and live life there so if they did make a mistake they could find the real guy."

At one point when Jane was citing yet another *CSI* episode, commenting "I am serious. I get all my stuff from there," Mike asked, "You know that's all fictional stuff you know." Jane replied, "I know. . . there's good stuff." She then went on to recount a story about a ten-year-old boy who killed his brother because he had told others about his bed-wetting. This was part of the discussion that had evolved from the question of different types of murder and different perpetrators.

Periodically, children are depicted as bad seeds in the media. This predates Columbine. As the population ages and adults are more distant from children, this is easier for audiences to accept. Children and seniors also compete for the same dwindling public resources and children do not have the vote.[5] Grossberg[6] also points out that since children represent the future, images of them often mirror the ways in which adults see the future. Children may be perceived as dangerous because the future is dangerous. *CSI*, in its search for bizarre plots on which to work its forensic science, often shows children as malefactors as do other crime programs such as *Law and Order: Special Victims Unit*. Low-income children have always been suspect. This is why child savers such as Charles Loring Brace[7] were eager to ship children out of cities on orphan trains to work in the healthy country air. Reform schools were also placed in rural setting to save children from the corruption of the city.[8] Situated as these two television programs are in cities and having as part of their allure the depiction of corruption behind the facade of civilization, they often show middle-class, respectable children as the villains. Given that both of these programs are particularly popular with children, the reflected image of children may lead to some concerns about how children perceive children.

At this particular interview, the children pondered whether there should be special laws for children who committed crimes. At what age, they considered did children understand the nature of their acts and how much were parents responsible if children got access to weapons. Examples were culled from various episodes to illustrate different variations of children's violent actions, reminding the children of programs that showed unbalanced adults. The discussion then moved towards mentally ill adults and the insanity defense, leading back to a concern about the death penalty. In an apparent demonstration of Piaget's[9] and Kohlberg's[10] description of the earliest stages of moral thought, the children echoed Roy's concern about the number of murders. Was a deranged mother guiltier if she killed five children or one? However, in a later discussion about torture, the children, who generally disapproved of the practice, examined the motives of those torturing prisoners. In the process of considering these issues, though there may have been traces of earlier moral thought, generally the discussions evolved towards complexity rather than simplification.

The questions that the children ponder as they consider the information they get from programs and the news suggest that new approaches to education are overdue. As children and adults deal with the flood of information and images available through television, movies and the Internet, they are challenged to think in new ways. Children's lives have rarely been as protected as the ideology of childhood stemming from the nineteenth and mid-twentieth century views of middle-class children liked to imagine. Although there are times when developmental stage theorists seem to describe children's maturation process accurately, the current view is that stage theory is a psychological construct. This view of childhood reflects a particular historical period.[11] According to this interpretation, literacy, as much as anything, separated children from the adult world, requiring schools to teach children how to acquire the new sources of information in print. The visual and aural media of television and film, as well as the unsettled nature of adult life, have bridged that separation. Just as children in earlier times took on greater responsibilities, so too do some contemporary children. Some of this is evident in discussions about the age when children should vote and work.

When asked to define a grown-up, Mike noted, "A grown-up is a big kid who thinks they can do better than their children and they probably can't."

Joe added. "They think they're superior because they are older."

The discussion continued as the children gave various ideas as to the age at which someone became grown up, ranging from sixteen to thirty. This led to the issue of the age at which children could work, a recurring theme, particularly for Roy who repeatedly asserted that he didn't know why children couldn't do some types of work. This moved on to whether people should get paid according to their age or how well they did the job. Agreeing that performance and not age should determine wages, the children then considered the right age for people to vote. Several noted that their parents did not vote, that they talked about it all the time, but never voted. Sarah felt that kids should be able to vote because they cared about the country too. This then led to a discussion as to what people needed to know in order to vote. Then Joe said, "I know this is totally changing the subject, but if a kid ruled the world there wouldn't be any wars."

Fred disagreed, but when Joe challenged him about the relative competence of adults, Sarah suggested that in regard to adults, "We have to give them a turn. They have been around longer."

"Some people are really good and they know what they are doing" Roy chimed in. "They're watching the earth. They're good persons. But then they have some people who go out every night and get drunk, come back home and they puke their guts out and then they go to sleep. I don't think they should be able to vote."

As everything does when talking with children, this led to an exploration of what was the nature of goodness ranging from caring for other people to not picking on them. When someone suggested that a good person did not carry a gun in his pocket, Mike as a hunter protested and they had to revise their definitions.

Children are able to observe the behavior of adults and of those among them whom they consider good from their own experiences as well as from the images that the media present to them. However, it is a question of whether they measure the media images against the reality and test the validity of those images or whether the media in its drama and repetition provides a model that is difficult to resist. Direct, daily experiences do not have the coherence that a shaped narrative does. The media continually offer compelling tales in programs, news and commercials.

A teacher reported that a fourth-grader on a class trip to the hospital exclaimed, "They have an ER, just like on TV." An anecdote such as this reflects the concern that many have about both children and adults. To what degree do the media shape people's understanding of the issues of war, the economy, and the society? Much of the literature about the media and democracy focuses on this problem.[12]

When the media are the major source of children's and adult's information about other groups, the audience may be aware on one level that they are viewing stereotypes, but on another, it may influence the way in which they organize their knowledge about others and their own lives and expectations. Certainly, politicians and advertisers believe that the stories they tell through the media will be successful in influencing people's behavior.

Using Goffman's[13] frame analysis as an operating principle, Kendall[14] examined the frames through which class was presented in the media over one hundred and fifty years. The New York Times was her primary newspaper source, while television programs and television news were examined as they offered ways of looking at class. There was a lens or a frame in which each class was viewed. The middle class to which most people in the United States believe they belong was the source of values, but the middle class was also perceived as victimized by both the rich and the poor. Evidence for her thesis might be found in the way children considered the poor in 2004 and 2005. In surveys in 2004 children wrote about them as the burdens on the middle class that Kendall describes as being the traditional frame the media presents about the poor. In contrast, the 2005 surveys had no negative comments about poor people, but only concern as they cited the aftermath of Katrina as one of the issues that needed to be addressed by the government.

Discussing television programs and not news programs, the interview children responded, "It doesn't portray them at all," when asked how television portrayed the poor. Rich people were shown as ". . . rich, snobby and mean." Responding to the question as to what ideas about women that they got from television, Sarah noted, "It depends what show you are talking about." On *CSI*, they are strong and know a lot. On *Family Guy*, they are evil according to the children.

There was also a range of responses to the question of how black people were shown. "They're all gangsters."

"They're nice."

"They are good at basket ball."

"They are stereotypes."

"They're not too many of them in cartoons; only one usually"

Other than this exchange there was almost no discussion of race. This was not surprising given the nature of their community and that there was no representative from another group. Still, in 2000, race was discussed more frequently as it was conflated with the issue of civil unions for homosexuals. Sexuality was another issue that was rarely raised directly by this group, except in regard to homosexuality. One time sexuality did come up, Roy had seen a program on the History Channel that disturbed him.

"Something that shouldn't be shown like I was watching about ancient Egypt or something and they said the youngest person to have a baby was a nine-year-old and I'm like never talk about it, never see it again. It's just a fact that is not a very good fact. It's just out there. It's. . ."

When asked about whether we shouldn't know about facts we don't like, he responded, "If we know that fact then we should. . . if we don't like it, then keep it to ourselves."

"But," Joe protested, "this is ancient Egypt."

"It's not offending anybody today," added Sarah.

Since the children, including Roy, had no difficulty describing in detail the violence they watched on television and in movies, their wariness around the issue of pregnancy seemed to be a combination of discomfort in discussing it in a particular context as well as of their own preadolescence. Why talking about a man raping and killing girls does not disturb Roy, but information about a pregnant nine-year old in ancient Egypt does may tell us something about his ability to see the difference between fact and fiction. One program was clearly meant to be entertainment while the other was presenting historical material. However, Roy's upset with the *CSI* episode in which the sexuality suggested some perversion indicated that fictional stories of a certain type were also disturbing. Considering that *Law and Order: Special Victims Unit* is devoted specifically to exploring sexual crimes, it may present an avenue for dealing with sexuality that may not be available elsewhere. However, if children do not have an opportunity to discuss these issues with adults, these programs may increase anxiety and misunderstanding. Crime programs may provide children with the vocabulary of the law courts as well as knowledge, however, fully or incompletely understood, about the law. Yet if the emotional sub-texts are not addressed, the information about sexuality, violence and other themes, will be distorted. The children have the ability to talk together about these issues and help clarify what they think, modifying their opinions as they listen to each other and to their own thinking.

These surveys and interviews show a group of specific children at a particular time responding to the issues and the media around them. Some of these issues have to do with their role as children in their families and their communities, even though they did not specifically address them. Where the children are socially and geographically has a great deal to do with how they see the world. They are children in a nation at war, but a war that in many ways is more distant than the battles they play out on their video screens. Their fathers tell them those video wars are false, but the children seem to have little more sense about the nature of real war than did the children in 1995 and 1996. They want the war to end just as children ten years earlier thought that the measure of a good president was keeping the country out of war. They probably have a better sense of the devastation that a hurricane can cause than that a war can. To some degree, this is because no matter where the children live, the major stories that the media send reach most viewers at the same time and in the same way, crowding out other stories. Stories are repeated, but not explored. The same images, the same phrases are cycled through the media. Although there are many television channels, they offer the same fragments of the news. There is no progression, no deeper understanding. The news is much like the commercials that advertise the same products with the same messages for the same length of time.

Children throughout the country see the war and Katrina presented in the same way. They also see other stories about children and families and crime and punishment, and although they can change the channel and look at other stories, reruns from their parents' childhood viewing, they will interpret them through the prism of their own experiences. In what ways do these various messages prepare children to live in a democratic society?

We have glimpsed what some of those messages may mean to some individuals, but what insight they might give us as to where children go with these ideas and emotions depends on a great many factors. The children will change as they move into adolescence, not only biologically, but in their status. The different expectations of themselves, as well as different expectations the society will have for them, will modify their concepts of the world.

As a society we are confronted with the problem of continuity and discontinuity in the preparation of citizens. To what degree does going to school, watching television, playing video games and doing research on the computer help children become members of a democratic society? How do all the messages fit together?

Democracy is constantly being redefined. Sometimes it is a rallying cry, sometimes it is seen as an illusion, but sometimes it is seen as a genuine attempt to create a society where there is equality before the law in spite of inequality in resources. Democracy can mean a society in which citizens act responsibly towards each other and their environments. Observing children struggle to define democracy is enlightening since adults without handy dictionaries might not be able to do much better than the children do talking about a system that is social as well as political. The children seem comfortable living in a situation in which they acknowledge that the government and the media betray their highly regarded value of honesty continuously. The children's cynicism may be superficial, a way to deal with their current situation, or it may reflect an acceptance of a reality that does not seem open to change.

How much will the children's ideas and actions change as a result of their physical and mental development interacting with the social and historical reality of their lives? At one point, I asked in the context of a discussion about people's behavior, whether they believed in change and whether they thought they would change. Roy laughed and said, "Oh yeah, we'll change. We got a pamphlet about that."

Notes

1. Steven Johnson, *Everything Bad Is Good for You.* (New York: Riverhead, 2005).

2. James P. Gee, *What Video Games Have to Teach Us About Learning and Literacy* (New York: Palgrave Macmillan, 2004).

3. Jean Piaget, *The Language and Thought of the Child.* (New York: Meridian Books Inc., 1960).

4. Susan Douglas and Meredith W. Michaels, *The Mommy Myth* (New York: Free Press, 2004).

5. Ann Crittenden, *The Price of Motherhood* (New York: Metropolitan Books, 2001), Lawrence Grossberg, *Caught in the Crossfire: Kids, Politics and America's Future* (Boulder, Colo. and London: Paradigm Publishers, 2005) and Sylvia Ann Hewlett, *When The Bough Breaks* (New York: Basic Books, 1991).

6. Grossberg, *Crossfire: Kids.*

7. Stephen O'Connor, *Orphan Trains* (Boston: Houghton Mifflin Company, 2001).

8. David Rothman, *The Discovery of the Asylum* (Boston: Little Brown, 1971).

9. Jean Piaget, *The Moral Judgment of the Child.* (New York: Collier Books, 1962).

10. Lawrence Kohlberg, *The Philosophy of Moral Development: Moral Stages and the Idea of Justice* (New York: Harper Collins, 1981).

11. William Koops and Michael Auckerman, eds., *Beyond the Century of the Child* (Philadelphia: University of Pennsylvania Press, 2003) and Allison James and Alan Prout, eds. *Constructing and Reconstructing Childhood: Contemporary Issues in the Sociological Study of Childhood* (London: Falmer Press, 1997).

12. James Fallows, *Breaking the News* (New York: Vintage Books, 1997) and Henry Jenkins and David Thorburn, eds., *Democracy and the New Media* (Cambridge, Mass: MIT Press, 2003).

13. Erving Goffman, *Frame Analysis: An Essay on the Organization of Experience* (New York: Harper Row, 1974).

14. Diana Kendall, *Framing Class: Media Representations of Wealth and Poverty in America* (Lanham, Md: Rowman and Littlefield Publishers, Inc., 2005)

Chapter Five

Books, Textbooks, and the Classroom

There is a value to analyzing more traditional sources of information along with contemporary media. That some children still find books interesting is exemplified by the comment a boy made about a Harry Potter movie, "Books are way better; like in the movie he just walks down the hall, but in the book you notice everything. You can hear the creaking." And as a girl added, "Books are better because you can read their thoughts."

A great deal has been written about textbooks as well as about some of the other books that children read that are a source of ideas and attitudes such as historical novels, biographies, picture books and comic books. Although this sample of children showed little interest in the comic book genre, its significance as a lightening rod of censorship and concern requires some examination, particularly as in its new form as the graphic novel, it is incorporated into school and pubic library collections for young adults. We have seen how movies affect children's ideas about the presidency. Books that are more highly valued as a medium by educators also need scrutiny. Studies about children's literature in Hitler's Germany and in the Soviet Union and China demonstrate how significant these texts can be.[1] In these instances, not only did the state see the significance of reiterating a particular message, but also in filtering out alternate messages.

As Postman and others[2] have pointed out, each new technology incites concern about its impact on children. Print has a long history of suppression. No political or religious position seems immune from this tendency to examine the "stories told to children." Ravitch[3] discusses the "political correctness" that emanates from the left and the right influencing the content of textbooks.

There is a paradox that needs to be confronted. On the one hand, censorship seems to be a dangerous vehicle to keep individuals, including children from thinking for themselves. On the other hand, we assume that the ideas that we encounter in various ways will have an effect on our behavior. Very few children or adults are likely to slavishly imitate that which they read in a book or see on television. However, attitudes may be shaped by what is read or seen. If we claim that reading and/or viewing broadens or narrows an individual's experience and understanding of the world, then the issue of what is or is not in books becomes relevant. This, however, does not need to lead to censoring children's reading as much as discussing some of the issues books raise.

Take for example the much beloved work of Dr. Seuss. As picture books tackle more complex themes, they are not relegated to the early years of childhood, but are often enjoyed by older children and used in elementary school classrooms. Seuss' work has many levels of readers. The messages that Seuss offers children are frequently thought provoking. *Yertle the Turtle*, *The Lorax* and *The Butter Battle Book*[4] make strong political statements about authoritarianism, ecology and pacifism. The tyrannical Yertle is unseated from his turtle-high throne by a burp from the turtle at the bottom of the stack. *The Lorax* is a sad tale of an environment devastated by greed, despite the warnings of the Lorax about overcutting the forest. Most depressing of all of Seuss' books is that of the escalating armaments race between those who eat their bread butter side up and those who eat it butter side down. Unlike most Seuss books, that, no matter how moralistic, usually end on a positive note, *The Butter Battle Book* leaves the future unresolved. From the celebration of the imagination that is *And To Think That I Saw It On Mulberry Street* where on his walk home from school Marco transforms a horse and wagon into a glorious parade to the anti-materialism of *How The Grinch Stole Christmas*,[5] Seuss coated his didactic messages in infectious compelling verse and nonsensical images. Seuss also undertook to transform dreary reading primers into playful verbal games using the limited vocabulary of beginning readers in his *Beginning Book* series.

Despite the many virtues of his work, one notes the lack of strong female models in his *If I Ran*[6] stories. Generally, in all of his books, females are passive. Cindy Lou Who in The Grinch is sweet, but hardly a role model. The narrator, as well as the major protagonist, in *The Cat in the Hat*[7] books are male. Even the female task of procreation is taken over from Mazie a lazy bird, by Horton the Elephant. The world of action is dominated by males.

Other adult readers might well be concerned by the anarchy that is celebrated in *The Cat in the Hat* books. Order may be restored at the end of the book, but clearly the joy comes from disturbing the universe. Although this worries the children in the story, they still find some enjoyment in it as does the child reader. Adult authority is continuously subverted in Seuss's work. We might applaud the positive messages that are presented overtly in his books while being concerned about the covert messages that accompany them.

This type of analysis is exactly what critics like Ravitch[8] deplore whether it is from religious fundamentalist groups or organizations like the now defunct Council on Interracial Books. However, parents, teacher and librarians have felt that their task has been to monitor children's reading both in terms of content and form. Although the religious fundamentalists have been among the most active groups raising objections to books, other groups have also protested what they feel is unfair representation of their experience. These protests have led to a greater inclusion of African American characters and stronger roles for women.

One of the easiest and most consistent of criticisms is the aesthetic one. Certain books, such as series books, are scorned as not being well written. However, there is an extensive literature extolling the virtues of Nancy Drew as a female role model.[9] Brown and St. Clair[10] credit The American Girl series of historical tales as the impetus for a renewed interest in juvenile historical novels, leading to the Dear America series among others. Christian-Smith[11] discusses the values of the Sweet Valley High books in developing discrimination among the various books in the series. Using the same principles that inspired Radway's[12] landmark study of women's reading of romance novels, Christian-Smith[13] investigated the meaning of the series to the readers rather than prejudging what they were gaining from them. The idea that children might develop their own tastes by reading a variety of literature is frowned upon by adults whose own reading may include books of questionable literary value.

Readers, critics, and scholars have debated what determines literary value for centuries. Is Shakespeare with his melodramatic blood and guts plots saved by the language in which the tales unfold? Is Dickens in a bound book more acceptable than the Dickens that was serialized in the nineteenth century? Do Black Mask writers acquire cachet when the Library of America anthologizes their work or comic books acquire dignity with the nomenclature of graphic novels? Today's pot boiler may be tomorrow's classic. After all, Stephen King received the National Book Award. Did it elevate him or lower standards as some claimed?

Given that these questions will not soon be resolved for adults, we must also recognize that in the name of childhood, adults in their various capacities have seen censorship and indoctrination as a responsibility and a duty. Politicians are particularly prone to pronouncements about protecting children from sex and violence, not by enacting laws that limit the businesses of pornography and weapons, but by castigating books, movies, television, video games and the Internet. The example of Fredrick Wertham and his crusade against comic books in the 1950s does not seem to make any impression on the next generation of adults. The fate of his particular mission should be instructive since many of the comic books he condemned have become collector's items. In championing new technologies, advocates often point out that the amount of time spent on entertainment remains the same, only the form changes. Given the sparse attention given to comic books on the sixth grade surveys, this seems to be occurring. The scorn allocated to comic books has shifted to video games that well may come into their own as an art form in the future.

A transformation seems to occur in individuals when they move from childhood into adult status. Just as the Opies[14] noted the difficulty that thirteen year olds have in describing the games of their youth, so adults seem to forget the pleasures of their own reading, claiming that what is published currently is much worse than what they read as children. Piaget[15] has pointed out that when one moves to another level of thinking, it is difficult to recreate an earlier one. This may explain some of the generation gap. However, it is also the case that not all of the concerns adults have for children's reading are altruistic, but are also concerned with questions of control.

One of the concerns about television has been its accessibility to the very young child who may not yet be in school. Children in the higher grades of elementary school often share that concern as the interviews in this study indicate. Given the proliferation of picture books for all age children, concern about their content can also stimulate controversy. The furor over Maurice Sendak's *In the Night Kitchen*[16] with its acknowledgement of male genitalia provides evidence of how vigilant librarians think they must be. Although initially not as overtly political as Dr. Seuss, Sendak focused on the subversive elements of childhood in *Where the Wild Things Are* where a child becomes angry enough to want to eat up adults. Sendak's *We Are All in the Dumps with Jack and Guy* depicting the plight of homeless children is a book that seems to be targeted at an older audience as was *Brundibar*.[17]

Certainly books having to do with sexuality arouse a great deal of anxiety at every age level as demonstrated by the reaction to *Heather Has Two Mommies* and *Daddy's Roommate*.[18] The intention of these books was twofold; to reassure children in homosexual families and to educate children in heterosexual families about the diversity that is possible in family structures. These two books were not necessarily designed for the preschool child. When included in the New York City public school Rainbow Curriculum, they caused uproar. Their picture book format may have made them easier targets than some chapter books dealing with the same subject. Like comic books, their combination of the visual and the verbal was disturbing. Aesthetically, neither book is noteworthy, but it would appear that few images have been more scrutinized or perceived as more threatening. Seeing gays and lesbians is apparently more disturbing than just hearing about them. An author, such as James Howe, popular with elementary school children for his Bunnicula books that recount the adventures of an enterprising hound, includes a homosexual boy in his book *The Misfits*.[19] He is just another one of a group of children who are the target for teasing in middle school. Aimed at children ten and up, this book is one of many that addresses topics that make adults uneasy. None of these books focus on the sexual aspect of homosexuality, but rather are trying to encourage a more understanding and accepting attitude towards families and individuals. Given the way in which homosexuality is used as a taunt in schools and on playgrounds, this might well encourage more acceptable behavior.

Inappropriate language is another stimulus for anxiety on the part of adults. No matter what the character's provocation, children do not swear in children's books without parents and politicians becoming irate. One of the major incidents galvanizing the local community in which these studies took place was around a book depicting two boys on a camping trip in Vermont. There were five offensive words, including a four letter one describing excrement. The local library was filled with parents, teachers, and concerned citizens. The schools had a widely used policy about children not being required to read any books that offended their parents. Such parents, however, are vigilant not only about their own children, but everyone else's as well. After a parent noted that the words were far less explicit than what appeared on the bathroom walls in the school, the policy was maintained.

Censorship is a political as well as a moral act. Almost twenty years ago, Demac[20] described the history of the repression of dissent in the United States from its earliest days with the Alien and Sedition Acts. Although John Peter Zenger's imprisonment under a British governor is cited as the stimulus to an exercise in freedom of speech in the textbook used in the local supervisory union, there is nothing about the Palmer Raids in the 1920s and McCarthyism in the 1950s. In both these cases, freedom of speech and political thought was challenged. From the first World War on, the anxiety about the impact of socialist or communist thought in the United States weakened first amendment rights. Something similar is a result of the War on Terror despite many groups that continue to fight to preserve this right. That this is an ongoing struggle would be useful for children to know as they are often restricted in what they can say. Many of the zero tolerance policies in schools could be seen as an extension of the idea that there is little difference between words and actions.

Even if children are not used as a wedge to curb political discussion, banning books for children seems to be an important exercise of adult authority. Given how little children seem to be reading, compared to other activities, one can only wonder whether there is a greater furor over books because they are more vulnerable and less profitable than other media. Children's major access to books is primarily through public institutions such as schools and libraries. Pressure has been exerted to have a rating system as far as films and television and video games are concerned, but these are media privately used by adults as well as children. Our surveys and interviews suggest that the ratings on these media do not hold up. Although Tipper Gore and Wal-Mart exert some control over access, it would seem that the market place is stronger than the censor, particularly when an older member of the family is involved.

In the past, particularly during the McCarthy era, television and movies through vehicles such as Red Channels identifying individuals who should be blacklisted felt censorship in their ranks. However, with the advent of cable television, videos and DVDs, the niche market seems to have diluted the impact of such attacks. Mickenberg[21] claims that children's trade books were always much less susceptible than textbooks to censorship. Even when books were banned in certain parts of the country, they were still in use in other places.

Certainly the phenomenon of Harry Potter provides an interesting example of the difference between film and books. Whereas some groups have banned the book, the movies are among the highest grossing films each year they appear. Witchcraft on the page seems more threatening than on the screen. The issue of witchcraft is a tangled one, having a history that comes from the middle ages when women's power was suppressed by depicting its source as coming from the devil. This is a tradition going back to the Garden of Eden where it was Eve who caused all the trouble in the world with the help of a serpent. WICCA was formed more out of a recognition of witches as a manifestation of the goddess principle, than necessarily out of belief in the supernatural. Satan, the Wiccans claim, is a Christian invention in which they are not interested. Yet, the major criticism against the Harry Potter books seems to reside in this idea of witchcraft, which is at best a metaphor in this unfolding tale of growth and empowerment. Can adults really believe that children will transform a wand bought at the local bookstore into a weapon as effective as one purchased in Dignon Alley? Perhaps it is the ambiguity involved in the fight between good and evil that troubles adults. J. K. Rowling[22] has made it clear that people are not necessarily what they seem to be and that even the best of individuals have their flaws. One wonders why fantasy that clearly delineates the boundary between the Muggle world and the Hogwarts world is so disturbing.

Although there have not been any reports of how specific minority groups have responded to Harry Potter, it is clear that this is a book with a wide base of child readership. It has become a book that belongs to children as well as to the booksellers and the merchandisers. On Kidspeak,[23] an Internet forum devoted to children's issues around freedom of speech and children's rights, there is a campaign for children to defend Harry Potter from the various accusations of witchcraft and violence that have been leveled against it. Children of all ages articulate their support although the fifth and sixth graders are somewhat concerned about the appropriateness of the book for younger children. They assert that they can tell the difference between fantasy and reality. Some of the children identify themselves as Catholics and, contrary to the new Pope's concern, assert that it does not diminish their faith.

Is it the witchcraft that disturbs the adults or are they, like J. K. Rowling, using it as a metaphor for the power it unleashes in children. When Harry breaks the rules, the children claim, it is only to achieve a greater good. Harry and his friends are fighting evil, and if the adults do not see as clearly as the children do, the children must take matters into their own hands, using powers that the adults have given them through their tutelage in the dark arts. There is an interesting sequence in *The Goblet of Fire*[24] when Hermione is concerned about the status of the kitchen elves and those who serve the school. There is the suggestion that she is being satirized for her political correctness, but she raises a disturbing point about the hierarchical system that supports the ruling class. Corruption is everywhere and as the series progresses, the simple dichotomy between good and evil becomes blurred. It is not only that one can not tell who may be an agent of Voldemort, but that the existence of Voldemort taints everything. This is a more complex morality tale than first appears.

Children may have great power in this account, but they are not the innocent children that parents wish to protect from the evils of the world. It is not just that Draco Malfoy represents all of the school bullies that haunt the imaginations and the reality of school life, but that this school structure mirrors the adult political system. The carefree days of childhood are not that as children will be quick to admit and which Rowling reveals to the discomfort of some adults. Schools do mirror the class system of the adult world with the favored rewarded with more than their share of popularity and admiration, as well as tolerance for their misdemeanors. Study after study of children's peer groups confirms what Rowling describes with such accuracy.[25]

As genres, children's fantasy and science fiction deal with the issues that are muted in the realistic fiction by the need to reflect the world in contemporary terms. Children however, know that it is not the presence of instant messaging in a book that makes it real, but the deeper conflicts that find so little expression in the schools. Is it because schools wish to convey the idea, as textbooks do, that everything is set and that the right answers have been confirmed?

Granted that fantasies offer children the opportunity to explore moral issues and to feel empowered beyond the confines of their condition, the genre may be more conservative than subversive. It is the gifted individual who restores order. He, or more rarely she, may lead a team to save a world that is usually more medieval in its structure than democratic. After all, the children do become kings and queens in Narnia.

Harry Potter is not the only fantasy book that has ruffled the sensibilities of the adult moral watchdogs. The Oz books, now considered classics, had their detractors initially. The nineteenth century seemed more comfortable with fantasy than the twentieth and the twenty-first even though the literary genre has flourished during this time. Certainly writers like George MacDonald used fantasy to convey moral lessons.

On the surveys, fantasy books were the most frequently cited as favorites. Some of that, of course, is due to the Harry Potter and Lemony Snickett craze, but other fantasy novels were also cited. Even though recently some fine science fiction books have been published for this age level, fantasy involving alternate worlds was clearly favored. There may be a tie-in with the current spate of fantasy movies such as *Narnia* and *Lord of the Rings* as well as the Harry Potter and Lemony Snickett movies. Supporting this idea, when children did mention comic books, Spider Man was named most often. The appeal of fantasy not only resides in its themes of good and evil, but in the powers that the protagonists possess. A feature of many fantasies and superhero comics is that other people are often unaware of the powers of the hero or heroine. For the relatively powerless this is a satisfying scenario.

The concern about how well children can distinguish between fantasy and reality may have its source in a greater awareness of how often adults may find it difficult to make this distinction. A greater understanding of the human psyche does lead to wariness about the stability of the mind. Fantasies powerfully evoke the simpler dichotomies between good and evil while also suggesting the complexities in the struggle of contending forces.

Fantasies, of course, are not the only genre dangerous to children's minds according to adult censors. As noted with picture books, sexuality, even in its normal manifestation of a girl's menstrual period in *Are You There God? It's Me Margaret*.[26] needs to be suppressed. Perhaps it is not just the n-word that exiles Huckleberry Finn from the classroom, but Huck's willingness to go to hell for friendship. Even *Memoirs of a Bookbat*[27] devoted to questioning censorship, might be condemned for its lack of sympathy for religious zealots.

Contemporary realistic novels deal with many hot button issues such as homosexuality, alcoholism, drug use, sexual and physical abuse and school violence. Novels about the impact of divorce seem relatively benign when compared to stories about rape and self-mutilation. Granted that many of the books with these themes are addressed to older adolescents, some of these issues surface in books for preadolescents. Like television programs, the Young Adult books are also available to the elementary school reader.

Generally, it is easier for the society to condemn such books than to deal with the reality of these problems in children's lives. Given that the control over what is read by children is a political topic, what are the political messages within books from which children need to be protected? Even though some informants make it clear they wouldn't steal a book, books do get stolen, or misplaced. Therefore, some consideration should be given to the content of books, remembering that children come to books as they come to other media, without a history. The messages of media created in one time may be different when absorbed in another time. Books may be less vulnerable to the effects of time than visual media are given the difficulty children often have in accepting the styles of earlier periods. Books allow readers to visualize their own worlds as they read. Students in the twenty-first century have no difficulty reading 1950s *Catcher in the Rye*[28] even if many of the topical references elude them. This may speak to the universality of some works as well as to the nature of a form that is verbal rather than visual.

In the sixties and seventies there was concern about the lack of images of African Americans in children's books and the damage that this did not only to black children, but to majority children as well. The political ideas within the Newberry Award winners have frequently been analyzed since these books are perceived as a standard of excellence in children's literature. Over the years what seemed to be a conservative bias has been modulated by books such as *Roll of Thunder, Hear My Cry* and *Bud, Not Buddy*.[29] During the Civil Rights movement and the War on Poverty, more attention was paid to increasing the number of books that depicted both the history and the contemporary experience of African American and other minority children. Yet even the preapproved and generally acceptable Newberry books have not be immune from criticism. *The Slave Dancer* and *Sounder*[30] were first hailed as breakthrough books describing a part of African American history, but later they were reevaluated and found by some to be more negative than affirmative. This constant reassessing is a part of the process by which children's literature stays meaningful.

Within children's literature there are many sub-categories so that the images that arise from historical fiction, realistic fiction, fantasy and science fiction may be quite different. The way in which different topics are handled at different times reflects the changing temper of the times in which a book is published. For example the Revolutionary War is handled quite differently in *Johnny Tremain, My Brother Sam is Dead* and *The Winter of Red Snow*.[31]

In the first there is a sense of the glorious mission of democracy. The triumph of World War II is echoed in the pages about the fight for freedom that is fought and won by those who champion the people. At the time of the Vietnam

War, children are presented with a different view where a Revolutionary soldier is executed by the military for political reasons. By the 1990s, series like The American Girl and Dear Diary were teaching American history through fiction in a more self-conscious manner. The Washington family is humanized and war is not just an affair of men but includes women. Where *Johnny Tremain* focused on the leaders of the Revolution, *The Winter of Red Snow*[32] acknowledges the contributions of the common soldiers. Although there might be echoes of Prince Hal walking amongst the men before Agincourt in this depiction of Valley Forge, the book's scope is much narrower and less ambitious than the Forbes work. The role of women and girls is also emphasized to a greater degree.

The war that most intrigues novelists for children and for adults, of course, is the Civil War, that crucible in which the nation's identity was formed to borrow the language of the time. Although all the books agree that slavery was an abomination, one wonders what other political messages children get from the many perspectives that the literature offers. Do children perceive all of the ironies involved in Richard Peck's *The River Between Us?*[33] In telling the tale of his father's parentage, the narrator does not seem to recognize the implications of this for himself of being born into a mixed race family.

What are the lessons, implicit and explicit, that children receive from children's literature? The aftermath of the Civil War in terms of the positions of African Americans in the United States is demonstrated in the spate of books about the Civil Rights movement that reemphasize the point that oppression is wrong. However, all of these books locate the conflict over these issues safely in the past. A book such as *A Stone in My Hand*[34] with its sympathetic portrayal of Arabs in Palestine addresses issues closer in time, if not in space, and generates its own controversy.

When we consider children's books, we need to keep in mind what books are being read by what children under what circumstances. Northern suburban children assigned *Roll of Thunder, Hear My Cry* with its story of a black girl growing up in the South, will probably respond to it differently than children in an urban ghetto as will children in a Southern community.

Books written in different time periods may reflect the social conditions and attitudes of the time when they are written, but children read them in their own time period. Interested in a topic, they may pursue it by reading a number of books without necessarily noting their publication dates. Popular books are often reprinted and covers are continuously updated to appeal to new readers. Much as television reruns are watched, books are read ahistorically. Just as *Catcher in the Rye* transcends time barriers, so do many children's books, particularly in the fantasy and historical genres because their settings are not time bound. Although *The Chronicles of Narnia* emerge from postwar Britain, the contemporary child probably focuses on the adventure, rather than the history. Considering this context in a classroom requires students and teachers to distance themselves from content to a degree and to focus on books as objects to be studied, not only for their stories, but also for their pedigree. Who is written about and who is not in the story may become significant elements in understanding what the story is telling readers about themselves and others.

In the 1970s after Watergate, there was a movement in the schools called Values Clarification. The idea was that children could express their ideas without there being any indication from the adult what the answer should be. All speech was acceptable as different points were debated and children listened to each other. This was partly a response to the political situation and partly an outgrowth of the research on moral development. Needless to say, the outcry against this educational innovation was strong and the movement, never widespread, quickly dissipated. Some traces of this idea remains in organizations such as *Facing History, Facing Ourselves*. Some of the web sites designed for children seem to be utilizing this idea with their ongoing polls and requests for children to submit their own ideas.

The purpose of these movements is to encourage students to explore and think about issues for themselves, an ingredient one would think was necessary in a democratic country. However, many critics of our current public school system believe that it is an input model rather than an output one that dominates educational practice. Legislation such as No Child Left Behind supposedly evaluates what students have learned. However, can standardized tests measure what children remember and understand? Constant testing sends the message that there are right answers. Filling in the appropriate response is not dissimilar from voting once every four years and feeling powerless for the rest of the time.

Children have a great deal to talk about as each Harry Potter book appears. They do not know how the books will end and what the implications are of what they already know. As each book unfolds, the reader has a better and deeper understanding of what the preceding events mean. Harry and his friends change unlike the unchanging story that is told through the textbooks that they encounter in classrooms.

Much has been written about textbooks. From the nineteenth century forward it seems as if textbooks have been presenting images and myths rather than raising questions. Many critics have noted the tendency for textbooks to simplify rather than complicate. In *Guardians of Tradition*,[35] Elson describes, among other myths created in nineteenth century textbooks, the image of the noble, doomed Indian that emerged.

Textbooks are, like testing, a big business. Four major companies control the industry. They are agents of standardization to the same degree that tests are. Unlike other nations that have a centralized federal system of education, education has been the responsibility of the states. However, the federal government has been moving education away from the diversity, and in some cases inequality, of state controlled education through court decisions such as Brown vs Board of Education and legislation such as PL 94-142, for equality of education for the disabled, Title IX mandating gender equality in sports, and No Child Left Behind. Although the major burden for financing these reforms still rests with the states, aid programs such as Title I also shape educational policies.

Textbooks and national assessments have been contributing to this movement. However well intentioned publishers may be, they are still in the business of meeting customer needs. The political nature of this becomes evident when states such as Texas and California affect what the rest of the country reads because they buy their books on a statewide level. The history of the political influence of pressure groups on textbook publishing has been well documented.

The story of Harold Rugg's social science textbooks is instructive.[36] A professor of history at Columbia University, his textbooks were popular and sold well throughout the thirties to schools until they were attacked in 1940 as being un-American. His focus on cooperation as a way of solving social problems was considered dangerous. He also presented a realistic picture of slavery and its aftermath. His general focus on the strength of the people making decisions was perceived as threatening capitalism. One of the complaints against Rugg was that the books, "tried to give the child an unbiased viewpoint instead of teaching him real Americanism."[37]

Not only does this type of censorship prevent certain perspectives from being presented, but it smoothes out all controversy or relegates it to the past. In his book discussing the teaching of history, Loewen[38] debunks myths starting with Columbus and including misconceptions about Reconstruction, labor, and the class system among other illusions. The central myth, he claims, is that of America's exceptionality. Americans are always the good guys according to the textbooks. Loewen does not want them to portray the United States as all bad either, but complex and every bit as challenging as an episode of *Law and Order*.

Lincoln's struggles with his confused ideas about slavery indicate how an individual can change through experience. Unless children understand the country's conflicts, they won't recognize what has been done and can be done to strengthen democracy. Loewen[39] points out that the United States is not the country it was in the eighteenth century, nor is the government a simple checks and balances mechanism. What the country has achieved that has been positive has been the result of efforts of individuals. He decries a history that says war broke out as if no one had responsibility for it. Nor does he want us to subscribe to the idea of inevitable progress. Environmentally, we are probably not better off than were the Native tribes who lived in harmony with the natural world before the Europeans descended upon them.

Loewen[40] is concerned that the misinformation that children receive will lead to the cynicism that was perceptible in the interviews and surveys of this study. As an historian, Loewen would like students to grasp how some problems were solved and some created. The idea that democracy represents a healthy exchange of different viewpoints is lost not only in history textbooks, but in science and literature as well.

The children reported that they "did democracy in the fifth grade." To investigate what they "did," I borrowed the textbooks used in the district. I was also loaned the sixth grade Social Studies textbook. In the sixth grade, they "do" world studies. Examining textbooks provides only a limited view of what the experience in using them is for the children. Unfortunately, I only received the textbooks after the surveys and interviews were completed. Reviewing them with the students would have been enlightening.

These textbooks were published relatively recently. *Build Our Nation* was published in 2000, *History Alive! America's Past*, 2001 *People, Places and*

Change,[41] the sixth-grade book 2003. Given that it is not unusual in some districts for books to be dated, this indicated that. although prepared in the twentieth century, they had made it into the twenty-first. Although we are cautioned not to judge books too quickly, even though children I have interviewed about books do judge books by their covers, a number of impressions immediately surface. First, except for *History Alive*, these books are heavy. At eight and a half by eleven inches, they are not books that can be easily or conveniently read. They are also colorful with many pictures and graphics of all types. Besides having sidebars and inserts to meet the needs of contemporary multi-tasking children who are used to interruptions in their television viewing, no topic takes more than two pages.

Numerous people such as content reviewers, educational reviewers, and teacher reviewers are involved in their production. Besides having six authors, *Build Our Nation* had fifteen consultants and thirty-seven teacher reviewers. That was more extensive than the other books. *People, Places and Change* had only three authors, ten content reviewers and twenty-four educational reviewers. However, they also list their editorial staff of thirty-seven

This does indicate the extensiveness of the investment in these texts. The diversity of the reviewers also suggests a serious commitment to diversity. For *Build Our Nation,* there were consultants from the Council on Islamic Education, The Institute of Buddhist Studies, Asian-American Studies, the Freedom Forum First Amendment Center, the East Asian Institute and various history departments. Geographical as well as academic diversity, was also evident, in consultants from the University of Texas, Harvard, Princeton, Southern Methodist University, University of Colorado and the University of California at Berkeley. Teacher reviewers were also from all over the country. The extent of the involvement of these consultants is not clear but from other accounts of the process of textbook publishing, it may be that their jobs were to check for accuracy and to avoid offensive stereotyping.

As the slimmest of the volumes, *History Alive!* has twenty chapters with a total of two hundred fifty-six pages including the index and acknowledgements compared to *Build Our Nation* with twenty-two chapters at seven hundred and six pages and *People Places and Change* at thirty chapters with seven hundred and fifty pages. Nineteen of the chapters in *History Alive* take the reader to the end of the Civil War. Chapter Twenty covers all the events from that point forward.

Beginning with the positive aspects of the text, there is some sensitivity to the experience of Native Americans and African Americans, although it does tend to put a good deal of responsibility on African tribes for succumbing to the Europeans desire for slaves. There is even some sympathy shown for Mexicans and Chinese in the process of securing the "Manifest Destiny" of the United States. Women's role, if not extensive, is at least referred to and the example of Deborah Sampson in the Revolutionary War is cited.

The book is profusely illustrated with information conveyed in the picture captions as well as the text. The chapters are all laid out in the same way. There is an advanced cognitive organizer that tells the students what they will learn, the material, a summary about what they have learned and a teaser to lead on to the next chapter. The chapters are relatively short; questions are included within them. There is usually a large picture on the left-hand page of each chapter beginning with smaller scenes excerpted from it with questions that leads one to examine the larger picture more carefully. Sections within each chapter are no more than a page long. There is some attempt made to focus on the lives of ordinary people, particularly within the Civil War chapter which focuses on the lives of soldiers and the problems that they faced on both sides of bad food, bad shelter and bad medicine.

The text even includes little known facts such as slaves joining the British during the Revolutionary War. This sensitivity to minorities may be the result of the number of consultants and reviewers they list. There are six contributing authors beyond the two main ones, two consultants, three scholars and six teacher reviewers. With extensive maps, a glossary, an index, acknowledgements of the pictures and appendices with the Declaration of Independence, the Constitution, the pledge, and the Star Spangled Banner, every thing seems to be covered. The amendments are explained in as much detail as can fit into a page with a picture on it in a chapter of its own.

Given its structure, the book is easy to read and probably is good with poor readers as some of the research on its web page suggests. There is a web page prominently featured on the cover. Except for some links to other pages, the page seems primarily a resource for teachers.

Four chapters are devoted to the Revolutionary War and the view of colonial life focuses on the English colonies. There are two chapters on the lives of Native Americans and they are referred to throughout, particularly in the two chapters on settling the west. There are visuals on almost every page, including maps, photos, paintings, charts, cartoons. The cartoons are not amusing ones, merely illustrations in drawings of a point. For example, the Civil War is explained in terms of a sister and a brother fighting over the sister's playing of loud music. This comparison is explained as a metaphor and the reader is enjoined to think about this metaphor as they read the chapter. The question is raised, "Does the brother have the right to change his sister's habit?"[42] This seems to be a shaky analogy since the answer could easily be no, she should just go to her own room, an argument that the Southerners were perfectly comfortable making.

There are also two contrasting pictures on facing pages; the left-hand side shows "The Colt factory, which produced weapons, was like many of the factories that began in the North."[43] Although relatively static and somberly tinted, it is clear that the factory dominates the landscape, dwarfing people and residences with little natural foliage. On the opposite page is a sepia toned picture of an idyllic scene of a large house nestled among trees and bushes, with a white man and woman foregrounded, a dog accompanying them. This caption says, "Plantation owners became wealthy as they used slave labor to plant and harvest cotton."[44] The previous spread showed a painting from the Library of Congress of a plantation in which there were a variety of workers in the fields, a black man lounging on a wagon, a dark man in the field on a mule, supposedly the overseer. There were two white people, again in the foreground, the man with his back to the slaves and the woman in profile. Four smaller pictures taken from the painting are at the bottom of the page, asking questions about what the people were doing. As a depiction of slavery, it is relatively benign despite what the text may be saying.[45]

As noted, the chapter entitled The Civil War focuses on the personal rather than the political and on only one battle, Gettysburg. Sherman's infamous March to the Sea is summed up in one sentence. "He (Grant) ordered General William Sherman to march from Tennessee through Georgia to the Atlantic Ocean."[46] Such bland statements will offend no one but they hardly do justice to the reality of the war, despite the authors' earlier observation about the war being fought primarily on Southern soil.

In the next chapter there is a photograph of Martin Luther King, Jr. and Malcolm X shaking hands. The caption accompanying the photograph reads, "Martin Luther King, Jr. (left) and Malcolm X (right) devoted their lives to ending discrimination against African-Americans."[47] Without class discussion or viewing of films such as *Malcolm X*, eleven and twelve year old students might never know that both of these leaders were assassinated.

Reviewing the previous nineteen chapters, it becomes clear that no one gets assassinated in this version of history. The Civil War ends at the Appomattox Court House before Lincoln's assassination. *Build Our Nation* does include Lincoln's assassination, as well as a paragraph reporting on the assassinations of President Kennedy, his brother and Martin Luther King. The final sentence of that paragraph is, "The assassinations were signs of the conflicts of these decades."[48]

This is better than the last paragraph in *History Alive!* on the page before the one page on The Information Age, which reads "The Civil Rights movement resulted in a number of laws that protect the rights of all Americans. It also inspired other groups to fight against unfair treatment, such as Mexican Americans and women."[49] However, one cannot blame students who think that everything was solved or that the various wars were akin to uninteresting episodes on the History Channel. Television appeals to children because of the conflicts it shows. American History is rife with conflicts, but one would hardly know it reading these texts. Granted the authors have done their best to show the history from multiple perspectives and their concern about informing students about Native Americans and African Americans, but it is history from the perspective of compassionate winners about unfortunate losers. Taking three paragraphs from the chapter on the Revolutionary war and changing the names and time might be interesting.

> Unlike the British, Continentals were fighting in their home country and could get supplies easily. As the war went on, the Continental Army found new ways of gathering equipment and supplies. Often, local citizens sold or gave the army food. Soldiers also captured cannons and muskets from the British.

Continental soldiers also had the support of women. Women ran the farms and businesses, while the men were away fighting. They brought supplies to camp, made uniforms, and worked as nurses.

In contrast the British had to fight in a country that they didn't know well. Most colonists refused to help them when they needed food or supplies. Often, the British felt surrounded by people who disliked and even hated them. These feelings made it harder to want to fight.[50]

Maybe referring to the Iraqi war would be too controversial, but the Vietnam War might provide some insight into how the United States may be perceived by others. Differences between the United States as an occupying force and the British would provide insight into the complexity of war that is not always a simple battle between good and evil, but between different perspectives. The differences in the nature of warfare because of technology might also be discussed. There needs to be ways to connect the eighteenth and nineteenth centuries to the twenty-first century for the study of history to be meaningful as a prelude to the present. Some sense that the current struggle between red and blue states has a history stemming from the Civil War might enable students to see history as something alive.

Build Our Nation seems to have benefited from some of Loewen's criticisms of texts in presenting a more realistic picture. The non-English colonies are discussed. Immigration and labor are featured in the chapters that deal with the history after the Civil War. However, since each of its sections is four pages in length, there is a limit to how much the text can accomplish. True to its mission of teaching democracy, it has sections on Citizenship that raise issues and offers suggestions for activities. It also includes selections from literature that liven and humanize the information. One of the skills workshops asks the students to compare primary and secondary sources. There are lesson reviews and chapter reviews. In the chapter reviews, there are creative thinking and writing assignments as well as project suggestions and activities. The authors attempt to balance vocabulary and fact exercises with more interesting and challenging ideas. There is also reference to an Internet option, Internet Social Studies Center. Checking on this reference led to an academic site that might not intrigue the students.

The visuals in all three textbooks are excellent. Pictures of students and quotes from them work on making a connection to the readers The art work is varied and engaging, but also distracting. Reinforcing a multi-tasking or attention deficit concept of the students, the texts suffer simultaneously from being too broad and too shallow.

There are some features in *Build Our Nation* that try to expand the students' views. One entitled, Turn the World Around,[51] asks students to look at the map from the perspective of the other countries in North America. There is also a Handbook for Learners that guides students through the various skills involved in reading maps and other graphics and organizing reports.[52]

Textbooks do not stand alone. They are one resource in a classroom that requires a teacher to work with a variety of materials and use it to generate the children's questions as well as those of the textbook authors. Summarizing the differences between communism and capitalism within a single paragraph makes it hard for young people to understand the intensity of the cold war. A definition of capitalism as, "**Capitalism** or free enterprise, allows individuals, not government, to choose their work and to own farms, factories and other businesses."[53] This does over-simplify the class system that the children may be aware of in their own lives even if they do not see it in their textbooks or on television.

If studying one nation over four or five centuries seems daunting, the sixth-graders must have the sensation of going around the world in eighty days when it comes to reading *People, Places and Change.* Each European nation gets four pages that consist of two pages of history, one of culture including religion, food and the arts, and one page describing where they are currently. Russia and China get somewhat more space. There are case studies interspersed with the descriptions and sections on Connecting to Art, Technology, Math, Science, Literature and History as is appropriate to the different nations. Again, there are stunning graphics, diverse activities and reviews. There is also a predictable pattern to the way in which information is presented. Granted that the students read the texts over a year's time and that predictability is the basis of all genre literature, there is a sameness that dulls the individuality of each of these nations.

Clearly, those producing textbooks are aware of those who have been making similar criticisms over many decades and many books. Within bounds, the authors and editors respond by increasing the number of women and minorities who are highlighted. Even so, because they do not focus on any topic with any depth, students can not fail to conclude that history is about past struggles that were not very important, "because" as one boy concluded, "eventually, they were all just going to come together anyway."

Textbooks, whatever their limitations or strengths, exist in the context of a classroom. Teachers can transform them into vehicles for critical understanding. They can supplement them with other materials, use them as a springboard to their own ideas about teaching, or they can ignore them. They can use them as a guide, or they can attempt to follow their chronology with devotion.

The classroom is a dynamic situation that is shaped by many factors. Any analysis of how the classroom, books or textbooks affect children's ideas and attitudes about democracy must recognize this. There is probably no workplace that has been more observed, discussed, or critiqued than the schoolroom. Individuals from differing political perspectives and social positions have contributed their analyses to the educational discourse.

Not only is the structure of the actual classroom hierarchical with the control in the hands of the single teacher, but the school and the system of education is as well. Teachers are as much controlled by the nature of the educational system as are the children. They do not determine the curriculum. Citizen boards at the local and the state level do by the standards they set, the regulations they devise and the funding they approve. Inequities in funding and its consequences for children's education has been well documented over the years.

Historically, schools in the United States, unlike those in European nations, were relatively decentralized with the greatest control in the hands of state boards of education. This led to a great deal of variation in the type and quality of education that children received throughout the country. Since World War II, however, there has been an increase in the role of the Federal government in terms of funding, and of often unfunded or poorly funded mandates. The latest manifestation of this is the No Child Left Behind act. Testing and uniform teaching materials such as textbooks also push education towards a more uniform practice and standard.

There are few fields that are more examined, or from which greater accountability is demanded. Yet, consistently, there are outcries of despair and indignation about the nature of children's learning. Reform movements are recurrent in education, leading to a certain cynicism on the part of classroom teachers. Lortie,[54] in his penetrating study of school teachers, notes some of the anomalies in the teaching profession. He questions designating it as a profession since teachers, unlike other professionals, have little control over the conditions of their work. They have relatively little control in determining the curriculum. Economically, it is front-loading, meaning that the initial pay teachers receive determines the level of their subsequent salary through negotiated increments. Doing the job well does not lead to greater economic success, despite many recent proposals to the contrary. Teachers are not certified by their peers, but are licensed by the state in much the same way as hairdressers. There is a high turnover rate in teaching. A physician who left his practice to go into real estate or to open a boutique would be considered quite unusual, but that may be an economic step forward for a teacher. John Goodlad[55] in his attempt to improve the quality of teachers' professional preparation, referred to this high turnover rate as detrimental to the society as well as to the individual. Sarason[56] also felt that teachers' lack of decision making power limited the education of children and harmed the society.

Until recently, elementary school teaching had been the domain of women who found the teaching schedule compatible with raising families. Although there have always been male teachers at the secondary school level, their presence at the elementary school in the past had usually been in the role of principal. That is changing. Although women are still in the majority in the elementary school, more men are also teaching at that level.

Unlike the media, schools isolate children from the experience of alternative adult worlds. Not that the media is as wide ranging as it might be. Detectives, lawyers and forensic pathologists are not the major workforce in this country. However, they do have relatively more autonomy than teachers, and more excitement in their daily activities. For at least twelve years, children and teachers live and work together in a system that is inherently undemocratic for both of them. Ironically, the only example of democracy in action they may see is the local community voting down the school budget to protect property taxes.

Segregation is another factor that undermines democracy. Kozol[57] has written extensively about the resegregation by race that is occurring, but segregation by economic class has always been a factor in education in the United States.

Funding primarily through the local property tax is one of the reasons for inequity in public schools. There has also always been a thriving private school system paralleling the public schools. How these differences manifest themselves is illustrated by a study that Anyon[58] did. She observed five public schools, sitting in on classes, focusing on the math lessons, but also observing other subjects as well. All of the classes were fifth grade and all were using the same math textbook. After defining social/economic status, she assigned schools to these categories based on her criteria. Two of the schools she designated working class schools, one was middle-class, one affluent professional and one elite executive.

In the working class school, the work was done by rote, with children following directions. There were no explanations of the principles behind the procedures. Rules for behavior were often arbitrary and not explained to the children. The children spent a great deal of time copying from the blackboard and listening to the teacher reading from the textbook. If they needed to leave the room, they had to get a signed and dated pass.

The middle-class school focused on the children getting the right answers, rather than learning by rote. However, textbooks were followed with little or no questioning beyond checking on whether the children understood the material they had read. Controversy in social studies was avoided. Rules were established by the school and the reasons for them were explained. The learning did not seem to have much relevance to the children's lives, but they were able to ask questions about the material, even if the answers were vague. The children were encouraged to do well and learn the various skills they would need for further education or jobs.

The last two schools, the affluent professional and elite focused on the children as individuals. The assignments in math and other subjects were creative, calling upon the children to think and organize. Children were encouraged to find their own solutions and disagree with the textbooks. Rules were negotiated between the children and the teachers. In the affluent school when children wanted to leave the room, they wrote their names on the black board and left. In the elite school, they could leave the classroom even without that. There was a different level of trust. The focus in both of these classes was on demanding a high level of independent work on the part of the students. In the elite school, students would take over as student teachers to present lessons. In these schools, there was none of the sarcasm and belittling that took place in the working class schools. Anyon[59] referred to these differences in teaching approaches and learning experiences as the hidden curriculum of class.

Certainly, there are always exceptional teachers in any setting. Gerald Levy[60] in examining the ways in which the structure of a ghetto school undermined the best intentions of educators, finishes his dispiriting analysis with the description of a teacher whose class overcame all of the obstacles he had just depicted. However, the structure of schools should be supportive of teachers and children rather than exemplifying the undemocratic aspects of the society at large. This idea that democracy is a balance between individuals of unequal power, protecting those without power as well as those with challenges the pervasive myth of equality that children encounter in their lessons and which they know from experience to be untrue. Facing the conundrum that a slave- holder wrote "all men are created equal" might invigorate classroom discussion. In fairness, *Build Our Nation* does note that "In 1776, not all people had the same rights. Only white men who owned property could vote."[61] The authors then note that African Americans and woman looked to the Declaration of Independence for the same freedoms and rights. However, they do not make it clear that Jefferson was a slaveholder. The children have to rely on comedian George Carlin to bring this to their attention.

For a world that engages them, children go to television, movies and video games and books like Harry Potter. The media, however, have their own educational pitfalls and their own myths. Presidential elections are presented as a contest between two personalities rather than an examination of issues. The conventional media wisdom is that people are not interested in issues other than social ones such as abortion and gay marriage. Talking with children suggests that this is not so. They seem fully aware of the complexity of contemporary life since in most cases their lives are anything but simple.

Notes

1. Christa Kamenetsky, *Children's Literature in Hitler's Germany* (Athens, Ohio: Ohio University Press, 1984) and Felicity Ann O'Dell, *Socialization Through Children's Literature: The Soviet Example* (Cambridge: Cambridge University Press, 1978).

2. Neil Postman, *The Disappearance of Childhood* (New York: Random House, 1983) and Joshua Meyrowitz *No Sense of Place* (New York: Oxford University Press, 1985).

3. Diane Ravitch, *The Language Police* (New York: Alfred A. Knopf, 2003).

4. Dr. Seuss, *The Lorax* (New York: Random House Books for Young Readers, 1971), *Yertle The Turtle and Other Stories* (New York: Random House, 1950) and *The Butter Battle Book* (New York: Random House, 1984).

5. Dr. Seuss, *And To Think I Saw It On Mulberry Street* (New York: Random House, 1937) and *How The Grinch Stole Christmas* (New York: Random House, 1957).

6. Dr. Seuss, *If I Ran the Zoo* (New York: Random House Books for Young Readers, 1950) and *If I Ran the Circus* (New York: Random House Books for Young Readers, 1956).

7. Dr. Seuss, *The Cat in the Hat* (New York: Random House, 1957) and *The Cat In the Hat Comes Back* (New York: Random House, 1958.

8. Ravitch, *Language.*

9. Betsy Caprio, *the Mystery of Nancy Drew: Girl Sleuth on the Couch* (Trabuco Canyon: Calif.: Source Books, 1992), Caroley Stewart Dyer and Nancy Tillman Romalov, eds., *Rediscovering Nancy Drew* (Iowa City, Iowa: University of Iowa Press, 1995), Sherrie A. Inness, ed., *Nancy Drew and Company: Culture, Gender and Girls Series* (Bowling Green, Ohio: Popular Press, 1997) and Bobbie Ann Mason, *The Girl Sleuth* (Athens, Ga.: The University of Georgia Press, 1995).

10. Joanne Brown and Nancy St. Clair, *The Distant Mirror: Reflections on Young Adult Historical Fiction* (Lanham, Md.: The Scarecrow Press, 2006).

11. Linda K. Christian-Smith, *Becoming A Woman Through Romance* (New York and London: Routledge, 1990).

12. Janice A. Radway, *Reading The Romance* (Chapel Hill and London: The University of North Carolina Press, 1984).

13. Christian-Smith, *Becoming a Woman*.

14. Peter Opie and Iona Opie, *Children's Games in Street and Playground* (New York: Oxford University Press, 1969).

15. Jean Piaget, *Judgement and Reasoning in the Child.* (Totowa, N. J.: Littlefield, Adams and Company,1969).

16. Maurice Sendak, *In the Night Kitchen* (New York: Harper and Row, Publishers, 1970).

17. Maurice Sendak, *Where The Wild Things Are* (New York: Scholastic Book Service, 1963), *We Are All In The Dumps With Jack and Guy* (New York: Harper Collins Books, 1993), and Tony Kushner, *Brundibar* (New York: Hyperion Books for Children, 2003).

18. Leslea Newman and Diane Souza Illustrator, *Heather Has Two Mommies* (Los Angeles: Alyson Books, 1990) and Michael Willhoite, *Daddy's Roommate* (Los Angeles: Alyson Books, 1991).

19. James Howe, *The Misfits* (New York: Atheneum Books for Young Readers, 2001).

20. Donna A. Demac, *Liberty Denied* (New York: PEN American Center, 1998).

21. Julia L. Mickenberg, *Learning From the Left* (New York: Oxford University Press, 2006).

22. J. K.Rowling, *Harry Potter and the Prisoner of Azkaban* (New York: Scholastic Press, 1999).

23. Kidspeak, < http://www.kidspeakonline.org/iq.html> (5, Aug. 2005)

24. J.K. Rowling, *Harry Potter and The Goblet of Fire* (New York: Scholastic Press, 2000), 363-384.

25. Patricia A. Adler and Peter Adler, *Peer Power, Preadolescent Culture and Identity* (New Brunswick, N.J.: Rutgers University Press, 1998).

26. Judy Blume, *Are You There God? It's Me Margaret* (New York: Bantam Doubleday Readers, Dell Books for Young, 1970).

27. Kathryn Lasky, *Memoirs of a Bookbat* (San Diego: Harcourt Brace, 1994).

28. J. D. Salinger, *Catcher in the Rye* (Boston: Little Brown and Co., 1951).

29. Mildred Taylor, *Roll of Thunder, Hear My Cry* (New York: Bantam Books, 1978) and Christopher Paul Curtis, *Bud Not Buddy* (New York: Delacorte Press, 1999).

30. Paula Fox, *Slave Dancer* (New York: Dell, 1973) and William H. Armstrong, *Sounder* (New York: Harper and Row Pub., 1969).

31. Esther Forbes, *Johnny Tremain* (New York: Dell Publishers, 1943), James Lincoln Collier and Christopher Collier, *My Brother Sam is Dead* (New York: Scholastic Book Services, 1974) and Kristiana Gregory, *Winter of the Red Snow* (New York: Scholastic, Inc., 1996),

32. Forbes, *Tremain* and Gregory, *Red Snow.*

33. Richard Peck, *The River Between Us* (New York: Dial Books, 2003).

34. Cathryn Clinton, *A Stone in My Hand* (Cambridge, Mass.: Candlewick Press, 2002).

35. Ruth Miller Elson, *Guardians of Tradition: American Schoolbooks of the Nineteenth Century* (Lincoln, Nebr.: University of Nebraska Press, 1964).

36. Joel Spring, *Educating the Consumer-Citizen: A History of the Marriage of Schools, Advertising and the Media* (Mahwah, N.J.: Lawrence Erlbaum Associates, 2003), Ravitch, *Language* and Demac, *Liberty.*

37. Mickenberg, *Learning,* 96.

38. James W. Loewen, *Lies My Teacher Told Me* (New York: The New Press, 1995), 29-65.

39. Loewen, *Lies,* 249-263.

40. Loewen, *Lies,* 293-305.

41. Sarah Bednard, Catherine Clinton, Michael Hartoonian, Arthur Hernandez, Patricia L. Marshal and Pat Nickell, *Build Our Nation* (Boston: Houghton Mifflin, 2000), Bert Bower and Jim Lobdell, *History Alive! America's Past* (Palo Alto, Calif.: Teachers Curriculum Institute, 2001) and Robert J. Sager, David M. Helgren and Alison S. Brooks, *People, Places and Change* (Austin, Tex.: Holt, Rinehart and Winston, 2003).

42. Bower, *History,* 185.

43. Bower, *History,* 186.

44. Bower, *History,* 187.

45. Bower, *History,* 184.

46. Bower, *History,* 204.

47. Bower, *History,* 213.

48. Clinton, *Build,* 572.

49. Bower, *History,* 213.

50. Bower, *History,* 134.

51. Clinton, *Build,* 604-605.

52. Clinton, *Build,* 609-627.

53. Clinton, *Build,* 560.

54. Dan Lortie, *Schoolteacher: A Sociological Study* (Chicago and London: University of Chicago Press, 2002).

55. John I. Goodlad, *Teachers For Our Nation's Schools* (San Francisco: Jossey-Bass, 1990).

56. Seymour B. Sarason, *The Culture of the School and the Problem of Change, 2nd Ed.* (Boston: Allyn and Bacon, Inc., 1982).

57. Jonathan Kozol, *The Shame of the Nation: The Restoration of Apartheid Schooling in America* (New York: Crown Publishers, 2005).

58. Jean Anyon, "Social Class and the Hidden Curriculum of Work" in *Childhood Socialization,* ed. Gerald Handel (New York: Aldine De Gruyter, 1988), 357-382.

59. Anyon, "Social Class," 380.

60. Gerald Levy, *Ghetto School: Class Warfare in an Elementary School* (Indianapolis, Ind.: Bobbs-Merrill Col, 1970).

61. Clinton, *Build,* 273.

Chapter Six

The New Media

Ivan Illich,[1] an educator most widely known for his thesis about deschooling society, claimed that there were empowering and disempowering technologies. Mass media like movies, television and radio in his view were disempowering because the audience was passive, while audiotape machines and cameras were empowering since they gave control to the individual using them. While one might argue about the nature of the viewing experience since viewers do engage in interpreting what they see, it is true that the viewer does not take an active role in producing film, television and radio.

Following that model, video recording machines and computers are vehicles that empower their users. Some would include the remote control as another way in which the individual has control by changing channels and muting commercials. The Internet as an extension of the computer also expands children's abilities to know about the world. Cell phones, Instant Messaging, iPods and other devices that allow children to control what they hear and when, fall into this empowering category as well. Video games' place on this continuum is debatable. While they involve interaction on the part of the player, choices are restricted depending on the game. When children learn how to cheat or circumvent the designated pattern, they have more authority.

In comparison with computers, the Internet and video games, television is hardly a new form of media. Television has been a part of children's lives for more than fifty years. Granted film is over a hundred years old and books several centuries. Still the availability of television to children makes it a powerful force in shaping some of their ideas. It was also the medium that the interview children discussed most frequently.

Although there are many aspects to children's relationship to the various media, our main focus is on how the media prepare children to live in a democracy. Schools may teach directly about democracy, but many of their structural features supply children with experiences that are inherently undemocratic if we posit that a characteristic of democracy is the right of individuals to have some say in the rules that govern them. Using that criterion, the media, particularly television, would be categorized as undemocratic. Most television exists to sell products. Public television was initially the exception to this, but as it increasingly enlists underwriters, the lines between them and commercial television are blurring. Their merchandising of products is another aspect of their commercialism. Public Access Television, an offspring of cable television, is probably the only genuinely democratic television available. Whether it survives is questionable, but it does provide citizens with an opportunity to make their own television and to see their local community boards in action.

As many[2] have pointed, out there is nothing innately undemocratic about the media. What has made television so is its concentrated ownership. The history of government policy in radio and television broadcasting on behalf of commercial interests is not new. The airwaves that might be perceived as a public resource have consistently been awarded to businesses. Just as in the nineteenth century the government ceded public lands to the railroads, in the twentieth, they chose a commercial model when they gave away the air waves through awarding licensing to large corporations.

From the Radio Act of 1927 to the Communication Act of 1934, the government chose private over public interests so that currently even the public interest doctrine has been weakened. The FCC, during the Reagan administration, lifted restrictions on advertising during television programs designed for child viewers. Steyer[3] and others deplored the government's giveaway of the digital spectrum in 1996. The limits on the number of media outlets one company can own have been relaxed so that "Six corporations own or have controlling interests in most of the American mass media today."[4]

The implications of this for democracy are of concern to many, particularly since commercial interests are challenging unrestricted access to the Internet. As an indication of how the limited ownership of news stations affects discussion of these issues, Steyer claims that the 1996 act received nineteen minutes of news coverage over the course of almost a year. Not only must candidates for political office pay heavily for advertisements. but news coverage of elections is limited.

> In the 2004 election, an average half-hour of TV news contained three minutes and 11 seconds of campaign coverage. 92% of the broadcasts contained no coverage of any local election, whether for the U.S. House of Representatives, state legislature, or a city or county post. In races for the U.S. Senate, campaign ads outnumbered news by as much as 17-to-1.7.[5]

Given these facts, it is quite amazing that the children were as well informed as they were. We will look at some of the television programs that the survey children noted as their favorites and what they said they had learned from them, as it relates to the issues of democracy. To some degree, television programs and the Internet connect since most of the programs have web sites. The two television channels with the most frequently noted programs, were not surprisingly, Nickelodeon and Disney, both of which have their own web sites. These were often the same sites that were cited as favorites in the question about web sites. Both of these channels and web sites are devoted to children and deserve special attention. However, the children did not restrict their choices to programs geared for children. Like the interview children, they enjoyed adult programs as well, particularly *Law and Order* and *CSI*.

A suburban girl noted that her favorite television program was "*Avatar: The Last Airbender* because it is filled with action, humor and drama." Responding to the question about what she learned from it, she wrote, "That the world depends on the people. Everyone. We decide about what happens in the world-peace-war, teamwork. We, all of us together can shape the world's future.[sic]"

A visit to the Nickelodeon web site[6] provided video clips from this animated program, biographies of the major characters, a message board, games, and collectibles. There were links to other parts of the site as well as advertisements and a reminder of the viewing schedule. There was also a place to vote for the Nick night you can't miss.

Like comic books and graphic novels, the story line of *Avatar* includes traditional themes. There are four nations based on the four elements of earth, water, air and fire. In each nation there are men and women who can manipulate the element of their country. They are called benders who utilize martial arts and magic. In each generation, there is one bender who can manipulate all four elements. He is the avatar who is reincarnated down through time. The Fire nation has started a war against the other nations. The nation of air seems to have been destroyed and Water is just holding on as the Earth tribe fights valiantly against the Fire Nation. However, Katara, the water bender and the only female character among the five major characters, along with her brother, discovers a twelve-year old boy who is the last airbender and the avatar. The characters are all in their early teens and each has his or her individual personality that resembles some aspect of adolescence. Aang, the avatar is mischievous, Katara is idealistic and her brother resembles a typical jock.

According to one thread on the message board, the usual viewer of this program is thirteen although one writer comments, "Ok but I think more older people like this show and wont post.[sic]" The program combines many of the elements for which Nickelodeon has become known. Not only are the wisest and most significant protagonists children, but there is humor, limited violence and healthy messages permeating the program without requiring the end-of-program moral messages that He-Man needed in his day. The art work is soft, suggesting the Asian sources of the tale, but without some of the exaggeration and bright colors of adapted Manga.

Although children in this study report little reading of comic books, the comic book sensibility is still with them, not only in the film adaptations of comics, but in the aspects of mythology that permeate programs like *Avatar*. A special individual with special powers will arise to lead the people in their hour of need. Sometimes he will have disciples. At other times he will work alone or as a member of a team. He is often reluctant to assume the mantle of responsibility as is Aang in this version. One can see this as a parable for growing up. The child, in this case the savior is literally a child, has hidden powers, or potential, that circumstances force him to recognize and employ in righting the wrongs of the world. Embroider this tale with familiar sibling rivalry themes and preadolescent humor; add the exoticism of the Far East with wise elders offering cryptic advice and another generation of children is enchanted with the promises that such a vision offers them.

Katara embodies the female principle. Despite having to endure some of her older brother's sexist slurs, she has her own powers. Not yet a completely accomplished water bender, she is also a chosen one, helping the younger, but more powerful Aang. Katara functions much like She-Ra did in relationship to He-Man. Where he was Master of the Universe, she was Princess of Power, Defender of the World. Like She-Ra, Katara is compassionate besides being strong. These recurrent motifs in television, films, comic books are reinforced by the games to which the children are directed on the programs' web sites.

For continuous children's programming cable television has become a potent force in the lives of children, offering a range of viewing possibilities throughout the day and week. There is no longer the Saturday morning ghetto that dominated the networks. Each of the channels devoted to children have their spin-offs in movies, toys and tie-ins with fast food restaurants.

Few channels have captured as wide and faithful an audience as the popular Nickelodeon. Guided by enterprising executives, Nickelodeon created a different kind of children's television, showing the world from the child's perspective. Nickelodeon has 56 percent of viewership in terms of cartoon programs, indicating that their strategy has had positive results. Since 1996, Nickelodeon has rated number one in daytime viewing. Although challenged by Disney. Fox and Warner, Nickelodeon still leads in the ratings although with not as great annual growth as in the past.

Beginning April 1, 1979 and billing itself as the children's network, Nickelodeon has captured a devoted child audience from the toddler to the teenager. When it started, it was the only channel exclusively for children. Besides cartoons and music and audience participation shows, Nickelodeon also makes movies to further develop their popular characters. Sponge Bob has morphed into toys, key chains, greeting cards and other paraphernalia, breaking out of the ghetto of children's cartoons. He has not yet caught up with Mickey Mouse but he has a similar anarchic appeal. Nickelodeon has siphoned children's television from PBS and Saturday mornings to create a world that engages children through its variety of characters and themes. Currently owned by Viacom, Nickelodeon occupies a unique place in children's television.[7]

In the last twenty years there has been a recognition of the children's market similar to that which targeted teenagers in the 1950s. Just as music, clothing and movies helped define adolescence for generations of adolescents, toys television and technology have changed the landscape for younger children. Combined with an increase of mothers in the workforce and earlier experience with peer groups, life for middle class children has changed in reality and in image.

Whether or not children have become more independent and resourceful as a result, they are certainly exposed to more information and stimulation at earlier and earlier ages. Nickelodeon reflects this change by its emphasis on smart kids who from infancy on enjoy more complex relationships and fantasies than their parents imagine. Their programs are the children's entertainment and mirrors of their fantasy selves.

Children can also grow up with Nickelodeon since it has programs aimed at a range of ages. One student said that *Zoey 101*, a Nickelodeon story about teenagers at boarding school, showed her how to "interact with friends at school." An urban female noted that it taught you "how to be a teen." *Drake and Josh* teaches that "you have to be responsible for what you do." Nick News takes on the significant such as Intelligent Design and the insignificant about what kids don't like about school. The segments, hosted by Linda Ellerbee, are brief, usually including young people expressing their views.

Given the extent of its offerings, Nickelodeon needs to be examined for its underlying themes and messages. From its inception the channel's executives saw Nickelodeon as a children's haven. Even its Nick at Night was targeting the nostalgia of childhood for adults without necessarily losing some of its child audience. Establishing and maintaining a clear identity as a children's channel, Nickelodeon moved from its designation as the "green vegetable channel," or good for kids, to a channel children felt they owned. Slime was part of the appeal. but so were the images of empowered children. Parents also trusted the network because it downplayed violence in both its programs and, when it finally accepted advertising, in its sponsors. Nickelodeon also matter-of-factly presented strong females and children from diverse racial and ethnic backgrounds

Some suggest that this emphasis on females may be due partly to its women executives. Given funds to develop animated programming and a Nickelodeon style, Nickelodeon's second president, Geraldine Laybourne, hired creative people like Arlene Klasky and her former husband, Gabor Csupo. In keeping with the station's identity of "us against them" children against adults, Klasky Csupo created *Rugrats* where children have a language and a culture of their own, unbeknownst to their parents. Klasky Csupo were also responsible for *The Wild Thornberrys* in which this idea of a communication that adults do not know exists is also evident in Liza Thornberry's ability to talk with animals. Symbolically, this reinforces children's actual experience of living in a different world from adults who don't always understand them.

Initially Nickelodeon was a station without commercials. When it began to run commercials in 1984, it avoided the program as commercial that was typical of network programs such as He-Man and Care Bears. Nickelodeon also avoided advertising for products such as Laser Tag that promoted violent action on the part of children. Since Nickelodeon was a channel that was a children's channel, the children's parents also had to have trust in the programming. Even now commercials for the channel tend to be for food products, toys and films. There are clear breaks for the commercials that tend to number three or four at a time. Some of those commercials are also for Nickelodeon itself. However, girls who have seen Liza of *The Wild Thornberrys* adventuring with animals will be invited to believe in the magic of Barbie or to get hip with My Scene dolls. The animals the girls relate to in the commercials are furry mechanical cats and dogs. Boys in the commercials are either by themselves, engaged in making things happen or more active and energetic in shared commercials with girls. Although this is consistent with advertising for children's programs generally, it is jarring to see it after watching Liza and Debbie solve problems while facing a variety of greedy villains, or seeing Katara extricate her brother and Aang from danger with her water bending.

Both *The Wild Thornberrys'* early popularity and its decline may tell us something about the transition in women's roles that exists in the larger society. Although there is talk about possible women as candidates for president and although two women have occupied the role of Secretary of State, the first woman to be nominated to the Supreme Court is replaced by a man. Women have become state governors in greater numbers, but still few in relationship to their population. and in Congress, women are far from providing equal representation by gender.

Another significant aspect of Nickelodeon is the degree of participation it encourages on the part of its viewers. Besides voting for President during elections there are ongoing elections on the television programs and the web site as there are on the Disney channel and web site. What does the claim that Nickelodeon makes that kids rule mean exactly? Where and how do they rule?

A frequent response by the children to the question about what is democracy is that it is a system where people vote for their leaders. How does the ongoing voting about favorite programs or characters help the process of democracy? On the Disney channel, children are asked to vote on East vrs West, *Mulan* vrs *Pocahontas*. One is reminded of the Burger King Bill of Rights that circulated in their restaurants during the 2004 election. "You have the right to have things your way. You have the right to hold the pickles and hold the lettuce" and so forth till it concludes, "You have the right to crumple this Bill of Rights into a ball and shoot hoops with it." Granted this appeals to children's sense of humor and fun, but it also trivializes aspects of democracy as much in the commercial culture does.

Nickelodeon tries to present wholesome lessons to children while also providing adventures, social commentary and humor. There is a similar quality to the offerings of the Disney Channel. From the cartoons to the live action programs, Disney creates a world with which children can identify. Although not as popular with teenagers as with younger children, many of its programs were cited on the surveys; often the channel was referenced and not any particular program.

The Disney Studios have a long history with television. Disney first appeared on television in 1950. In 1954 the one-hour long, weekly, evening television program debuted and lasted for twenty-nine seasons. Much of the initial programming was extended commercials for Disneyland. In 1955, the Mickey Mouse club kept its target audience busy before dinner. Despite all of its various holdings devoted to adults, such as Miramax, Disney has primarily sold itself as the children's purveyor of fun and entertainment. In this tradition the Disney Channel went on the air in 1983. As was Nickelodeon, the Disney Channel is primarily commercial free. It does provide brief messages from its sponsors such as Kellogs and Dannon, but these are fleeting. Most of the commercial breaks are filled with promotions for other Disney programs, the web site, Disney and Pixar movies. Children interview stars from Disney films and television programs. Since the breaks are all about Disney, the question arises as to why there are any breaks in the programming at all. Does this suggest that children can not sustain attention for longer than eight or ten minutes? Or will the programs be sold to other channels that have conventional commercials? Is the Disney Studio generously allowing for bathroom and food breaks or is it reinforcing the conditioning of viewers of commercial television for stories to be regularly interrupted?

When children report that they learn how to be teenagers by watching *That's So Raven*, or that Fox's *Grounded for Life* teaches "life skills and how real life really is," the power of image over reality is suggested. As Kendall indicates the same stories are told over and over again on the situation comedies, on the dramatic programs and on news programs. In many ways, these stories echo the stories told in textbooks. American life is good, primarily middle class, blacks and whites get along together as do Asians. Like Raven, *Zach and Cody*, and the other adolescents and preadolescents who inhabit these worlds confront the same trivial problems that generations of television children before them have endured. They may be more hip and more racially diversified, but they are still trying to elude clueless adults, outwit obnoxious peers and deal with pesky siblings. At least, the Power Rangers were saving the world in between dances and football games. When the children migrate from children's programming to adult shows they find that crime is really the country's only problem.

What do children learn when they watch their favorite *CSI* and *Law and Order* programs? Integrated race and gender teams of devoted professionals work tirelessly to capture the evil doers who could be anyone, even children. The police's job is to give the lawyers evidence that can not be broken down in court, even if they have to tread on the edges of the law to do so. Defense lawyers stand in the way of the truth with their tricky questions and objections on procedural grounds. Everyone is guilty and must be proven to be so. The only miscarriage of justice is when the defendant goes free. Not to worry, however. There is a good chance he or she will be shot in the court hallway by an enraged victim. It is true that in the first half hour of the *CSIs*, the initial evidence may point in the wrong direction, but further evidence will correct that since the evidence never lies, is always meticulously collected and is never misused. On *Law and Order*, since the cops only have the first half-hour to catch their criminal, they rarely make such mistakes.

Stories on television are heavily patterned. It is as though children and adults were perpetually sitting around the campfire in Plato's cave, watching the same shadows dancing on the wall. There are few surprises in these stories, which is a part of their comfort. Like genre literature they reassure us with their sameness. Even the comedians who seem to suggest different perspectives are playing their role. It is a compensatory one to make the audience laugh at the rich and the powerful. They may have everything but they are still ridiculous in ways that the viewers are not. Even in this high tech age, the banker slipping on a banana peel is funnier than a little tramp doing so. Sometimes, however, the stories inadvertently change.

When we consider how the surveyed and interviewed children in 2005 spoke about the poor in contrast to the opinions expressed in 2004, we glimpse the power of the images they see and the stories they hear. Besides a year, all that separates the two groups of children was the depiction of Katrina on television. Whether temporary or not, there was a shift in their thinking. This was not a story about the undeserving poor. This was a story of the abandoned poor and the callousness of the powerful. Not only did this event underscore how strongly people respond to television, but it reinforced the concerns of those who think that democracy is weakened when the media is concentrated into the hands of just a few story tellers.

Contemporary technology initially seemed offer the opportunity to provide a more equal access to knowledge and information. Television was first seen as a potential classroom offering all that was best to the people. The Internet has inherited some of those dreams of universal access and control, not just by a few, but by many. Unlike some other countries, the United States made the choice to go the commercial, rather than the community or common carrier route with television. The struggle is now focused on the Internet with increased advertising on sponsored sites.

Just as technology might have shifted relationships among adults, it seemed to have changed the power relationships between children and adults, at least to a limited degree. Not only because children may be more comfortable with computers, cell phones, game boys and web sites, having had them as a part of their lives at early ages, but also because they provide easy access to knowledge that was previously denied them. Democracy emerged from a print culture. The reason why franchise was restricted was to some degree a matter of literacy. This is why it became a crime to teach slaves to read and why women's education was limited. Television provides not only a visual but also an oral culture. Ideas may be conveyed as they were in Plato's time through discourse. However, the assumption in an oral culture was that there was an exchange and that listeners were active and potential speakers, unlike the mass audience that absorbs the various televised messages. If the brain has become newly wired as some claim, what impact does this change have on the practice of democracy?

In arguments about children's rights as well as about the definition of childhood, much is made of the lack of experience and knowledge that are a part of children's dependency. Through technology the ratio of direct and indirect experience is changed for everyone. Citizens do not encounter a president in person, but they see him regularly on television, hear him on radio, read about him in the newspapers. And, as Myerowitz[8] points out, they look at him more closely than they could look at anyone in person. They are able to detect mannerisms and quirks. Responses are not always intellectually rational, but emotional. That there may be a social rationality to these observations can not be denied. This is why politicians are so concerned about their image. The image becomes part of the reality.

To some degree children share this experience with adults. Although within the first two years of life children still need the nurturing care that children of this age have always needed, these children are targeted by technology and taught early to respond to various cues. Part of this is the result of the research on the brain and the popular idea that since children are learning from birth onwards, this learning can be accelerated through exposure to the media. Therefore, there are Infant Shakespeare videos, Teletubbies and smash and bang computer programs for the very young.

Despite the efforts of well meaning adults to limit young children's exposure to the problems of the world, it is difficult for them to escape the images that confront them from a variety of sources. Television may be neutered to some degree, but as Katrina demonstrates, reality sometimes seeps in. The Civil Rights Movement owed much to television. Now, those children able to manipulate the Internet in a variety of ways, can gain control through contact with others and through their own actions. Although video games, like comic books, are usually talked about in terms of their most extreme examples, younger children will encounter *Pajama Sam* and *Carmen Sandiego* before the felons of *Grand Theft Auto*. They will also be bombarded with the games that the Disney and Nickelodeon channels urge on them.

An interesting aspect of some video games is that there are various ways to win the game depending on the choices that the player makes. Gee suggests that this might be a methodology that schools could follow. Children in this study, discussing school, thought that there had to be different methods for different learners, particularly those that were having trouble catching on. Their complaint was that school kept teaching them the same things in the same way even when they were not grasping the material. There have been authors other than Gee who believe that education needs to adapt to the new technological experiences of children. Others have felt that traditional schooling had not gotten it right long before the advent of television and computers. One of the aspects of Gee's work that is particularly interesting is that he undertakes to learn a new skill in playing video games. This does not often happen with adults who tend to rely upon the learning that they have to sustain them. This may be one of the factors that increases the gulf between children and adults.

Scarre[9] talks about the difficulties in incorporating younger generations into democracy. He approaches the problem somewhat differently than others do. Like Heilbroner[10] he does not focus on the structure of institutions as much as on the status of dependency. Democracy, he claims, offers its citizens free choices. Those choices are constrained by economic conditions he and others recognize. However, he says the problems posed by children have been too little examined. Ideas of democracy are based on assumptions of a static rather than a developing and changing state. Young people are absorbed into a status quo with little power to make any changes in the existing structures. As Spring[11] expressed concern that democracy has dwindled into a choice among consumer goods with the government being just another product, so Scarre[12] is concerned that traditional theories of democracy are limited because they do not suffi-ciently consider this issue of youth. It is not just the dependency of infancy that presents the problem as Heilbroner suggested, but the on-going subservience of youth that requires modification. After all, liberal democratic theory emerged from a society that wanted to assure that white men would be freed from the domination of the aristocracy. In schools not only do children have relatively little say over their learning, but in many cases they see teachers who are simi-larly constrained by textbooks, regulations and legislation. No wonder children relish worlds in which they can be in control. Harry Potter represents what every child dreams of being, an individual with unrecognized powers and potential beyond that of the adults around him. He knows what is important to learn and what battles need to be fought, as does every video game player. Do standard-ized tests and textbooks, rather than fantasy novels or video games, undermine children's learning?

While avoiding romanticizing these genres since many of their messages may be distracting or falsely reassuring, it is worth noting another aspect that the games and books provide. Unlike the bland histories that locate all conflicts and problems as safely past and resolved, these playthings of the mind are full of deception, treachery and danger. Gee[13] points out that one of their advantages is that one can lose and die many times without consequence other than having to begin again. Failing is an acceptable part of on screen life, whereas failing in school is often stigmatizing. Just as Dreeben[14] claims that one of the values of team sports is that they make collective failure acceptable because the team will try again, so does the video game offer a similar benefit. While adults strive to maintain children's innocence, children seek out the dark side to test themselves against it.

Gee makes the point that in playing video games the player depends on oth-ers even in games that are not on-line games. Through various web sites the player can access the knowledge of others or even develop variations on the game. In a way this empowers children, as tests never do, while also undermin-ing the idea that cooperation is cheating. Why shouldn't children share their knowledge? Why not learn from each other as well as from the adult? As con-temporary ideas of democracy emerged from the social conditions of the seven-teenth and eighteenth centuries, so contemporary schooling emerged from the industrial model of the nineteenth. This over-simplification is not meant to dis-miss the complex histories of democracy and education stretching back to before the Greeks, but it is to recognize that in both these cases, it was the extent of democracy and of education that changed the dynamics. Institutions arise from social conditions and the models of those societies become embedded into the institutions. An obvious example of this is the lecture, arising from the limited access to printed knowledge in the renaissance. In an age of books and comput-ers, the lecture makes no sense other than as entertainment. Writers like Papert[15] and Gee try to point education towards the future while politicians, well inten-tioned or not, chain children to the past.

Although the idea that education might be fun is a frightening one for some adults, Gee points out the amount of time and effort that is involved in learning to play a computer game. In many ways the procedure echoes the drill and skill exercises that bore many children. They may respond differently to video games because the rewards in video games are more immediate and more geared to the level of the player's ability. The computer is non-judgmental and adjusts to the actions of the child. Over and over again Gee extracts learning principles from the video game experience. Examining why individuals persist in certain behaviors can increase our understanding, not only of those behaviors, but of the dynamics behind them.

Although there are not many popular games that specifically teach the nature of democracy, there are some games that do. Positech Gaming[16] offers the game *Democracy* in which the player, in order to stay in power as president or prime minister, must get 50 percent of the vote. A Google search turned up 12,900,000 hits in 0.17 seconds to the words video games plus politics. There are Islamic games and games from Palestinian and Israeli perspectives, not to mention classics such as *Ethnic Cleansing* and *Custer's Revenge* whose titles convey their content. Although *Custer's Revenge* has been banned, it represents a type of game that is still prevalent in terms of extreme political content.

As the students talked about how the *Oregon Trail* taught them to think about allocating resources, these games allow players to participate directly in the current as well as historical conflicts. Many of these games are not rated for children. However, like videos, DVDs and CDs, games come into a household through the adults who do not always keep children from them. This again raises the question as to who has the authority over children's consumption of popular culture, the state or the parent? Although there are circumstances under which parents' rights may be terminated, such situations are not always clear cut and probably do not apply to most of the households in which children live. The issue of censorship is a complex one, not easily resolved, and one of particular interest to young people. Should parents have rights over children other than their own? The issue that was relevant in terms of printed material is equally volatile with games and web sites although the sums involved in the merchandising of such products is greater than with that of books.

There are numerous web sites specifically devoted to children and politics. Some of these web sites such as Kidspeak[17] engage students in expressing their ideas about issues such as the censorship of the Harry Potter books, as well as informing them about other instances of censorship. Kids Voting[18] is another site that encourages students to voice their preferences and ideas about more than celebrities.

Among the Internet sites that both the surveyed and interviewed children listed as favorites, striking by their absence were the many sites set up for children to teach them about democracy and the government such as bensguide.gpo.gov/, kids.gov, kidsvotingusa.org and whitehouse.gov/kids. Those interviewed had never heard of the sites and showed no interest in investigating them. Unlike the control that adults have in the classroom, the Internet allows the children to make their own choices. They may, however, be influenced by the incessant reminders on the television channels to visit Disney and Nickelodeon sites.

The most popular site was addictinggames.com, a free site with a range of different games at different levels. The interview children suggested a range of sites, some of which were also cited in the surveys. Funnyjunk.com, runescape.com, miniclips.com, candystand.com, funnypart.com and fart.com among others. When they were asked if they were to make a video game or a board game about democracy, what would it be like, Mike said they had made one last year in school. Joe said that its name was *Democracy Monopoly*. Evidently, this was a board game because Sarah suggested that it should be a video game in which to move to the next level, you answered a question. The children preferred a video game to a board game because the video game made noises. Roy said, "That gave me an idea. You have to work your way up in the democracy; then you start out as like this nobody and then to get to the next level you have to get voted as the person. You just keep going up." Earlier, Roy had explained Dungeons and Dragons that he played regularly with other children in his class, having learned it in Boy Scouts.

Responding to his idea, the children made various suggestions. Jane said, "Start out as Schwarzenegger."

"He was an actor, He didn't start our as nobody," Sarah protested.

Referring back to the game, Roy said, "Yeah, and if you made a bad decision, you got sued."

As they continued discussing the game, they agreed it should be like a *Sims* game. Three of the eight played *Sims*. Unlike the children on the survey, some of whom indicated that they played *Grand Theft Auto*, these children averred that they followed the game ratings. Roy made it clear that his mother insisted on that. However, when they later discussed music, they disagreed with the idea of a rating system. They also did not think that video games, music and television affected children's behavior. "It's like Cinderella. It's never real."

Based on the responses of the children interviewed in 2004, they may learn more about democracy and politics by extrapolating from their favorites. Just as they reasoned about the Iraqi war from those games, a suburban male in 2006 noted that his favorite video game, *Civilization Three*, taught him that "a nation must hire a good leader to move on."

Although on one level, most children know, as do most adults, that the games they play and the television they see are not real in the same way that school is real, they also recognize that it is more vivid. The patterns and the direction of their thinking are influenced by the repetition of themes and story lines. Becoming a *Roller Coaster Tycoon* or setting up a store on Disney's web site may be fun, but it is also reinforcing ideas about capitalism and work. Unless one specifically searches out such games, there are no easily available games about unions or cooperatives. As with television what is absent is as important as what is present.

Although many games are played on the Internet, that is not its only use for children. They use it as a source of information and of communication. All of the girls from the three different localities, rural, urban and suburban reported that 15 percent played video games a lot, while 26 percent used the computers, and 20 percent instant messaged a lot. For the boys it was quite different; 45

percent of them played video games a lot, 36 percent used the computer a lot and 17 percent instant messaged. Since many games are played on a computer and not on a console, one might infer that the use of the computer was in addition to the game playing. In comparing the localities by combined males and females, there is a striking difference between the suburban children and those in the rural and urban populations in this study. Seventy-three percent of the suburban children used the computer and 58 percent instant message, while the figures for the urban children are 34 percent using the computer and 32 percent instant messaged a lot. For the rural children the figures were 32 percent used the computer a lot and 14 percent instant messaged a lot. Given that the number of rural children was greater than the number of urban and suburban, this difference may be a function of the different economic resources available to the different groups of children.

A Kaiser Family Foundation[19] study found that children still spent most of their media time watching television, making the point that the use of the new media of the computer and video games did not displace video viewing, but was added to it. This dominance of television viewing seemed to be true of the girls in this study, 39 percent said they watched television a lot, while only 36 percent said they were on the computer a lot and 15 percent said that they played video games a lot. This was not true for the boys where 41 percent reported they watched television a lot but 45 percent said they played video games a lot. For the boys, the dominance of video games is confirmed by their responses to sometimes and not much. Forty-one percent of the boys said they played video games sometimes, and only 14 percent said not much. For television, 36 percent of the boys watched sometimes and 23 percent indicated not much. With the girls, the figures for video games were 35 percent for sometimes and 50 percent for not much. Girls indicated that 42 percent watched television sometimes and 19 percent not a lot. The boys and the girls were fairly evenly matched on instant messaging with 20 percent of the girls saying they did it a lot and 17 percent of the boys checking a lot.

In terms of listening to music, the boys were fairly evenly divided. Thirty-eight percent said they listened a lot, 31 percent said sometimes and 31 percent said not much. The results were different with the girls where 50 percent said they listened a lot, 41 percent said sometimes and 9 percent said not much. Boys reported using the computer somewhat more than girls did, although the differences were more between the heavy users. For those who used the computer sometimes, the boys and girls were much closer in their usage. Despite all of the variations, it is clear that a great deal of children's time is spent with various media. This seems supported by the small amount of time children of both sexes report working on a hobby. Forty-five percent of the boys and 39 percent of the girls answered not much in terms of hobbies.

Therefore, the percentage of children who report playing outside with friends is somewhat surprising. Fifty-six percent of the males and 50 percent of the females indicate that they play outside with friends a lot. Combining the a lot and sometimes responses makes the popularity of this activity clearer. The figures then would by 88 percent for the boys and 85 percent for the females. The surveys were completed from Fall, 2005 through Winter, 2006 so warm weather was not a factor in this result. Although one must be cautious about inferring too much from these results given the relatively small numbers of children involved and the nature of the questions asked, it does seem that children are absorbed in a world of peers and of the media. Piaget[20] did maintain that children learned morality from the peer group because of more equitable power arrangements. Whether that translates into more democratic experiences would have to be explored further. Given the extensive literature on peer group bullying and hierarchies, the results might be more salubrious in terms of physical activity than of models of democracy.

The rapidity of the spread of the new media and their extensiveness creates a situation for children with unique features. Although the new media are analogous to the old, they are more pervasive. In some ways they offer opportunities for children that might seem to be more democratic than the relationship of children to society has been in the past, recognizing that the past is more complicated than most of our stories about it suggest. If by democratic we mean providing children with the means to affect their own lives, to make responsible decisions and to be active members of a society in which rules and obligations make sense to those governed by them, it probably requires more than the media to bring about such conditions of autonomy.

In all the surveys and interviews in these studies, two ideas about democracy seem to dominate. The first is the importance of the vote, even though many political scientists think that the vote is only a part of what determines how a society functions. The second is the dominant figure of the president. This latter may be attributed to the experience of childhood and what has been a persistent feature of political arrangements with monarchs and other leaders filling the parental role. That the media enhances these two ideas is evident not only in political campaigns, but in the stories it tells of families and organizations. These stories have been modified by the media with the shift from the father knows best types of families to those where father, if not an idiot, is still often outsmarted by mother and children.

Another shift is the move towards individuals working together on dramatic shows to solve crimes and bring justice. Unlike the lone gunslinger of the Western film, the contemporary world is made right by members of groups bringing their expertise to bear on a problem. There still are leaders, and they may be brilliant and cranky like *House*, but they operate within the frame of teamwork. This may be the result of a marketing strategy to appeal to as wide a demographic as possible, but companionable groups suggest the emphasis on peers that children experience within their own lives.

However, it is not just the content of the media that is influential because along with the dramatic, comedy, and cartoon programs, children do see the focus on the importance of the president reiterated constantly. Although the old media of television was easily accessible to children in a way that print was not and also opened worlds of information to them, it still was controlled by adults who scheduled programs in order to sell products to the widest audience.

The new media of the computer and the Internet promised children the opportunity to be in control of what they read, saw, and played and when. They were also not immediately identifiable by their status as children, their race, gender or economic class. Their skill with the new technology was advantageous. Children become multi-taskers, listening to music as they instant messaged while muting the commercials on their favorite television programs. Obviously, not all children had these resources. Nor in many cases did the Internet offer any more edifying fare than did television. Children were allowed to vote and to express their ideas. During the last presidential election, the Nickelodeon message board overflowed with comments from children about the candidates.

On non-election years the opportunities, although there, are not as focused. Voting on the commercial web sites such as Nickelodeon and Disney tends to be trivial. When asked at what age people should be allowed to vote, many of the interviewed children suggested earlier ages than eighteen. Given their access to information through the media, this might make sense. However, the turnout for voters aged eighteen to twenty-for year olds is low. Some observers feel that the media are responsible to some degree because they increase cynicism among the young. There were certainly indications of mistrust of the government and politicians by the children in these studies as a result of what they saw on television, in films and in newspapers.

The media are not reliable messengers. The problems with television news are well known even to children who receive information from it. However, the Internet may also require a knowledgeable participant since many of the errors of the other media can easily be duplicated on the Internet. Just as television was going to revolutionize the classroom, so was the computer. Children seem fated to forever be enrolled in imperfect classrooms. If democracy requires an educated citizenry and the media are part of this educational process, informally and formally, what is to be done to enable children to use the media effectively to support, rather than subvert, their learning about the democratic process?

Notes

1. Ivan Illich, *Tools For Conviviality* (New York: Harper and Row, 1973).

2. David Buckingham, *The Making of Citizens: Young People, News and Politics* (London: Routledge, 2003), James Fallows, *Breaking the News: How the Media Undermines Democracy* (New York: Vintage Books, 1997) and Victor C. Strasburger and Barbara Wilson, *Children, Adolescents and the Media* (Thousand Oaks, Calif.: Sage Publications, 2002).

3. James P. Steyer, *The Other Parent* (New York: Atria Books, 2002).

4. The Free Expression Policy Project, <http://www.fepproject.org/factsheets/mediademocracy.html> 2, (6/27/06).

5. Free Expression, http://www.fepproject.org/, 4, (6/27/06).

6. <http://ww.nick.com>

7. Heather Hendershot, ed. *Nickelodeon Nation* (New York and London: New York University Press, 2004).

8. Joshua Meyrowitz, *No Sense of Place* (New York: Oxford University Press, 1985), 268-304.

9. Geoffrey Scarre, ed., *Children, Parents and Politics* (Cambridge and New York: Cambridge University Press, 1989), 100.

10. Robert I. Heilbroner, "The Human Prospect," *The New York Review of Books* 20, no 21&22 (Jan 24, 1974): 21-34.

11. Joel Spring, *Educating the Consumer-Citizen: A History of the Marriage of Schools, Advertising and Media* (Mahwah, N.J.: Lawrence Erlbaum Associates, 2003).

12. Scarre, *Parents and Politics,* 94-114.

13. James P. Gee, *What Video Games Have To Teach Us About Learning and Literacy* (New York: Palgrave Macmillan, 2004).

14. Robert Dreeben, *On What Is Learned in School* (Menlo Park, Calif.: Addison Wesley, 1968).

15. Seymour Papert, *The Children's Machine: Rethinking School In The Age of the Computer* (New York: Basic Books, 1993).

16. Democracy—The Ultimate Political Strategy Game <http://www.positech.co.uk/democracy> (5/22/06)

17. Kidspeak < http://www.kidspeakonline.org/ > (8/5/05).

18. Kidsvoting < http://www.kidsvotingusa.org/>   (7/17/05)

19. Victoria Rideout, Donald F. Roberts and Ulla G. Foehr, "Generation M: Media in the Lives of 8-18 Year Olds" (Menlo Park, Calif.: A Kaiser Family Foundation Study, 2005).

20. Jean Piaget, *The Moral Judgment of the Child* (New York: Collier Books, 1962)

Chapter Seven

Educating for Democracy

To the question on the survey of how they learned about democracy, children had a range of responses. Some offered more than one category; others indicated that they didn't know or that they hadn't learned. One child wrote, "By living in America." By and large, however, the responses fell into four categories. There were thirty-eight responses that said teacher. Ninety-three were school related such as Social Studies, books, dictionaries or a class trip. Twenty-nine indicated the media including educational television or simply TV, the news and movies. Family related sources such as parents or siblings were cited nineteen times.

Formal learning about democracy is probably associated with school since the children's lessons are specifically named in school. Children often indicated the grade in which the subject was taught, as did the interviewed students. A few of the survey children even noted that they had learned about democracy in school, but had forgotten what it was about. Granted that, it is surprising that television outweighs the family as a site for learning about democracy. Since studies show that children spend six and half-hours a day with some type of media, and two and a half-hours with their parents, the result should not be surprising.[1] When Steyer[2] refers to the other parent, he is probably not underestimating the power of the media, even if family may have more influence than children are aware of as is suggested by some of the interviewed children's comments over the years.

Before television and video movies, children's responses to political events generally moved from their neighborhood to ever widening vistas of state, nation and the world. Connell[3] points out that now children, while still young, indirectly experience global events in their own homes. Thus they come early to know about and react emotionally to those events which are most distant from them and least susceptible to influence exerted by the people around them. There is no chance for a sense of mastery or control to develop in the smaller local context before the person comes into contact with events and issues more difficult to affect because at greater remove. An important aspect of the charitable appeals to help victims of disasters such as Katrina is that by doing something tangible, the sense of helplessness that children may feel is alleviated to some degree.

As public schools were challenged by problems of poverty, continued segregation, the charter school movement and rising numbers of children diagnosed with emotional problems, Columbine and 9/11 increased anxiety among those responsible for children's well being. Adults were convinced that the way to combat potential violence was to develop zero tolerance policies and metal detectors in schools. Even in the relatively peaceful environment of the rural school, visitors must be checked in. However much these steps may have reassured parents about the safety of their children, they also functioned to further convert schools into prison-like environments where adult authority and power were conspicuously displayed.

Children, however, have not always been observers of political events. During the Civil Rights movement, African American children played a heroic role in desegregating schools. Indeed, it was his effort to understand the courage of Ruby Bridges that led psychologist Robert Coles to his extensive five- volume study of children, *Children of Crisis.*[4] Children were activists by going to schools that were hostile to them. Other children who historically felt politics directly in their lives were the so-called Red Diaper[5] babies whose parents were either Communists or involved in politically suspect organizations. These were children that during the McCarthy period in the 1950s had reason to fear for themselves and their parents. Recounting their experiences later in their lives, many noted that when the Rosenbergs were executed, they felt threatened for their own parents. At the other end of the spectrum are Lamb and Lynx Gaede, thirteen-year-old twins who since they were nine have been singing at neo-Nazi group rallies extolling white supremacy. Home schooled by their mother, these blonde blue-eyed, girls " . . . just want to preserve our race."[6] As a demonstration of their beliefs, they insisted that their donations to victims of Katrina only go to whites.

As indicated in several of the interviews, children may become more sensitized to politics when they perceive their families to be in vulnerable positions. There is also evidence that families with strong religious convictions tend to have children who become more involved and informed about politics. However, the survey results echo the conclusion that Hess and Torney[7] came to in their study of political socialization. The school seems to play the strongest role in informing and shaping children's political ideas, more so than most parents. Part of this may result from the trust that children have in teachers and their daily contact with them throughout the school year. The interview children made it clear that they believed their teachers more than they did television newscasters.

However, Hess and Torney[8] claim that because teachers avoid controversial topics, just as the textbooks do, the focus becomes on the compliance aspects of citizenship and less on the responsibilities of citizens. Indeed, young adults do report that they feel that their schools failed to prepare them to become informed voters. Just as the students are constrained so are the teachers by state and national standards and curricular mandates.

The teachers whose students participated in the survey also filled in questionnaires. There were ten teachers, five males and five females. Their teaching experience ranged from one year to thirty-five with the median at ten years and the average at fourteen years. Given the smallness of the sample and the variety of teaching experiences, the points of agreement among the teachers may carry greater weight since one might expect more diversity. Those from the rural schools, for example, were fairly consistent in explaining that the focus of the sixth grade curriculum was on other cultures even though the sixth grades did take a trip to the state's capital. Within that context, they did some teaching of democracy as exemplified by this response.

> Civics is not really part of my curriculum. I usually incorporate what's happening in the news-elections, scandals, and war and apply it to our country's philosophy of governance. It's more of a here and now approach. It makes it real and more meaningful.

The teachers in this district used the *People, Places and Changes*[9] textbook. One of them also mentioned *History Alive*.[10] The teachers from the urban and suburban schools did not mention the names of their texts, but indicated that they used them and supplemented them with a variety of other materials. Only one of the first year teachers in the rural school district indicated that he used the textbook as a supplement to other materials.

The sixth grade teachers in the rural district had a problem with the questions about their goals in teaching democracy and whether those goals related to the state standards. Since democracy is taught in the fifth and eighth grades, they could only address the subject indirectly as they were teaching about other cultures. The teacher in the suburban school noted that his state standards required teaching about the evolution of Democracy in Ancient Greece in May.

When asked what helps or hinders their goals, the consistent answer was time. There was too much to teach in too little time. One teacher commented, "Too much time testing, so since 'democracy' isn't tested in sixth grade, then it doesn't exist."

All of the teachers used media in their classrooms and generally saw them as effective as supplements and enhancements to the curriculum. Their views on the children's use of the media outside of the classroom varied more. Some saw limited value in the children's experience, while others felt that it provided them with some political information or raised some issues for them that were useful. Video games were singled out as a negative influence because of their violence. When asked about a media literacy program, three teachers did not answer, one was not sure, three were interested if the program was a quality one while three were very specific about the type of program. Years of experience was not a factor since one of the first year teachers did not answer the question as was true of a teacher with thirty-two years experience. However, the teacher with thirty-five years experience named a specific program and the other first year teacher wanted "Any program that combines valid information and integrates several types of learning styles."

There have been almost no funds from the national or state governments to support media literacy teaching. Some professional development money may be available to provide teachers with the skills necessary to implement a program. Many educators object to adding another subject to an already overcrowded curriculum. Others feel that an emphasis on popular culture is redundant since children are already sufficiently involved with the material.

Advocates of media literacy programs counter that it is not an additional subject, but rather a critical thinking skill that can be incorporated into other aspects of the curriculum. They feel that learning a visual grammar is as important as learning a verbal one. Reading Paul Revere's image of the Boston Massacre not only makes history relevant, but also demonstrates how arousing emotions has political consequences. Popular culture can also be a starting point for a discussion of the issues that video games, television programs and web sites raise. After all, there is a series of Popular Culture and Philosophy texts for college students with titles such as *Superheroes and Philosophy: Truth, Justice and the Socratic Way* and *Harry Potter and Philosophy: If Aristotle Ran Hogwarts.*[11] Even without such tomes as guides, Harry Potter is a rich source for media comparisons with films and video games. Those interested in media literacy want to move beyond condemning the media to showing how they work and affect people's ideas and actions. As is evident from the interviews, children themselves use the media as tools with which to think.

There are a few basic ideas driving media literacy programs. All media are constructed. Their messages are produced with particular goals in mind whether it is to sell products, to educate or to proselytize. The media present particular viewpoints and values. They are effective because of the techniques that they use to appeal to viewers. The emphasis is on the emotional, not necessarily the rational. Audiences bring their own experiences to their responses to the media. Children in a rural state watching crime dramas set in New York or Las Vegas will interpret what they see differently than will the children living in those locales.

There are a variety of media literacy programs. Some are easily accessible through the Internet, but most teachers could probably devise their own. Since all of the reporting teachers use the media in their classrooms, they may be already taking the first steps if they ask questions, not only about the content, but the form. Many teachers select information and show it in different formats so that the children may see how the presentation affects the audience reaction.

Just as media literacy needs to be a part of education at all levels from preschool forward, so should there be courses and programs as part of teacher education so that teachers will have the necessary skills and resources to develop programs for their students. Being able to analyze and evaluate the various means of communication is necessary for students living in a multimedia world.

Critics of media literacy seem to fear that if children understand the economic structure and motives behind the media, they will become disillusioned. Listening to the children discuss commercials and political broadcasts, that seems to be happening already. With knowledge, children are more likely to appreciate the technical skill that creates different effects and explore distinct ways in which such techniques might be used for better ends than continuous merchandising.

Some schools encourage student production of the media as a way to gain greater understanding of the various forms. Photography, video recording, audio recording, writing and editing all have their uses as long as children are not funneled into merely becoming technicians without sustaining the critical and creative approach necessary to make sense of the multi-media world they inhabit. The focus should not be on vocational training, but on an ongoing understanding of the potential and limitations of the media.

Critical thinking is an essential tool in all aspects of education. The techniques that the children learn in a media literacy program may be applied to literature and social studies classes. Recognizing the race, gender and class position of the creators of dramatic and comedic programs, news and commercials can help students see the agendas that are a part of any information. Students can then evaluate the reliability of the source. Analyzing written materials may be a part of children's experience in literature and social studies, but articulating the unique techniques used in visual and aural media will alert students to the various ways in which different media persuade their audiences. Buckingham's observation that the students with whom he worked focused on form rather than content indicates that the tools of analysis may be easily expanded and developed.

Students will also become aware of the voices that are not heard, their own amongst them. They may find that they want to offer a different portrait of childhood than the two that the adult world creates of the demon and the angel. Just as they may learn that different audiences may see the same program from different perspectives, they may find out that people, including themselves, tell stories from a variety of vantage points.

As necessary as a media literacy program is, it alone will not prepare students to become citizens of a democracy. If children's experience currently is one in which the schools and the children's status in society reinforce the conditions of dependency, then we do not, as a society, seem to be preparing them adequately for their role as future citizens. If children are actually not limited by Piaget's[12] topology of cognitive development, but can on certain levels reason in ways not too dissimilar from the ways of adults, as Matthews, Donaldson's and others works[13] indicate, how does a society provide experiences necessary to move children forward?

There first must be the sincere desire to undertake this mission. Schools, like the media, reflect society's values. Despite all the ongoing critiques of the schools, do they not change because the society actually values the service they provide? Early in our country's history, literacy was thought important for children so that they could read the Bible, then so they could be responsible workers and then so that immigrant children would be Americanized. Schools in the United States are constantly being reinvented, but not necessarily to meet the needs of the children. The Child Labor Law was passed in 1936, not for the benefit of children, but to protect the adult male working class from being undercut in wages. If secondary school students sometimes feel as if they are being warehoused, there may be some truth in that. Often the interviewed sixth-grade students wondered why there were some jobs that were not available to them for pay.

The question has been raised as to why children in the United States don't learn when so much time is spent teaching them. Reports on how little our students know are constantly presented to the public. This is often used as evidence that the public schools have failed and that their funding should be cut if they don't improve. Why is it that children in this study had difficulty naming the Governor and the Senators of the state, but no problem in naming the team of pathologists on *CSI*? Or if they were taught about amendments in the fifth grade, why couldn't they remember what one was in the sixth grade? One obvious answer is that the children were more involved with *CSI* than with state government. For them democracy may be located sometime in the colonial past as it is in their textbooks. They were well aware of the President and the Secretary of Defense because the result of their actions was evident to them, not only in the media, but also in the high gas prices of which their parents complained. Roy was very much aware of the war protesters who gathered every Saturday morning at the town's Four Corners. He understood their purpose.

The children may not be well informed, but they are not stupid. Nor are they uncaring. When the survey children were asked what would be the first thing they would do if they were in government, only seven out of two hundred and eighteen responded that they would do away with school. Most of the answers were thoughtful ranging from meeting the needs of the poor to ending the war in Iraq. There were many that were concerned about controlling drugs and smoking and other social problems. One reply that stood out was, "Um, I'm not really sure. The first thing would probably be to think about what I should do."

One of the aspects of a study like this is that when I asked questions, I did not know the answers. The children were aware of this and generously shared their expertise. In the textbooks, the authors ask open-ended questions to get the children to think. However, there was no place for the children to ask questions. The children asked me questions and gave me assignments as to the web sites I should investigate and quizzed me on my reactions. At one point they asked me why I was doing the study. I replied that I thought children were smarter than most people gave them credit for. The children were surprised. "Wow," Roy said, "Someone on our side."

Most teachers are on their side, but they have many pressures on them, such as the No Child Left Behind Act, that I didn't have. Part of the reason that the children feel that the teachers are worthy of the trust they have in them is because these are adults, more than their parents, with whom they spend almost as much time each day as they spend with the media. Teachers are not perfect, but children learn how to relate to them, what their strengths and weaknesses are, what they will let them get away with, and where they will draw the line, what they care about.

The community may not permit teachers to engage children with the controversial issues that the media does, but it can not stop them from embodying certain values. To understand teachers and children, it is necessary to live within a classroom, to experience the ebb and flow of a day, the excitement, the boredom, the tension, the laughs. The power of teachers has always resided in their classrooms where they can decide how to convey the mandated lessons, what to emphasize and what to forgo. This is limited power, however, because the United States decided that citizens would control education, not the professionals. The scorn that some politicians heap upon teachers and the word "professional" may be the residue from their own days as powerless children. Being without power, even within the most benign of classrooms, can leave its mark.

Although teachers can shape the day-to-day experiences of their students, they also have the experience and the expertise to contribute to framing the context for learning. Textbook publishers wisely have teacher consultants, but they are few in number. Communities need to find active roles for teachers in deciding on content and assessment. Vermont has a history of teacher and community involvement. In the 1970s, under the leadership of Commissioner Harvey Scribner the state undertook to craft the Vermont Design for Education. Emerging out of countless meetings with parents, teachers and community members, the Design defined the educational goals that would guide the curriculum. In the 1980s, the focus was on Public School Approval where once more the communities, including the teachers, worked to set standards that included everything from the school facilities to the necessary assessments. In the late 1980s and early 1990s, the state again undertook a review of its schools. With Richard Mills as the Commissioner, Vermont moved towards Outcomes Based Education, as did many states. The state also pioneered in the use of Portfolio Assessments. Standards were high. Teachers were consulted and helped to shape the curriculum goals. These various changes were not completely accepted by all teachers who felt, with some justification, that there were too many changes too quickly. There was, however, a commitment at the state level to involve teachers in the process. Many participated enthusiastically

Vermont also formed a Vermont Standards Board for Professional Educators. This twenty-three member, teacher majority Board is a policy making board, appointed by the State Board of Education. The Board oversees relicensing of teachers and administrators as well as approval of higher education teacher education programs. In 2003, two pre-service teachers were added as non-voting members in order to be sensitive to the needs of future teachers.

In 2006, the Vermont Society for the Study of Education commissioned a study on teachers' attitudes about No Child Left Behind.[14] Dana Rapp, an associate professor at the Massachusetts College of the Liberal Arts surveyed two hundred and sixteen Vermont teachers. According to the study 80 percent of the teachers felt that No Child Left Behind did not reflect students' needs and 93 percent of those surveyed felt that the children's love of learning had been lessened. Ninety percent disagreed with the current Commissioner of Education that the law wouldn't harm Vermont schools. Other findings in the study addressed classroom issues such as the limiting of class discussions, less engaging intellectual activities and more worksheets and teaching to the test. The way in which this national mandate superceded the reform movement in Vermont probably reinforced some teachers concern that the educational winds constantly shifted and were beyond their control.

If the United States wants to improve education, not to mention to prepare children to be citizens in a democracy, it needs to rethink its attitudes toward teachers. Perhaps this will only happen when the experience of children in a classroom change and misplaced resentment about their dependent state is not all laid on the back of teachers. Not having school budgets dependent upon local property taxes would be helpful. Still, there need to be ways in which teachers can have more say about policy issues. If their presence as members of local school boards would create too many problems, they could be members of Advisory Committees whose recommendations would be seriously considered as they were in the development of the standards and curriculum in Vermont. When we show respect for teachers, the message is not lost on the children. For their own survival children are careful watchers of adults and what they value. They clearly and early know the relative status of teachers and baseball players.

Just as teachers need upgrading of their status, so do children of each economic and social class. During the 1970s, poor children were quite visible in the educational and developmental literature and in the awareness of the general public. They now have vanished into different categories of immigrant children, emotionally disturbed children, children in single-parent households. Even Head Start, a remarkably sturdy program, is slowly being budget cut to extinction. But however they are designated, poor children like middle and upper class children need to learn how to be citizens.

From Anyon's[15] description of the different classrooms as well as from much other documentation, it is clear that children of different classes receive a different education. It is instructive to see what are the parameters of an education designed for the country's future leaders are like. There are smaller class sizes, more resources, well-designed and attractive buildings and better-paid and more experienced teachers. For years, it has been a well-known fact that local property tax school funding leads to higher expenditures at a lower tax rate for wealthy communities and lower expenditures at a higher tax rates for poorer communities. Although the courts in various states have ruled against this inequity, states have not been successful in solving the problem. In those cases where we do not have segregation by race, we do have it by class.

Theoretically, No Child Left Behind addresses this problem, The Charter School movement also claims that by closing failing public schools and allowing parents to have a choice, poorer children will have more opportunities. In some cases this may be true, but the results seem to be mixed and not guaranteed. Statewide funding is resisted because many communities feel that the only governmental service over which they have any genuine control is their local school system. That control is weakened by federal educational mandates accompanied by inadequate funding. In the 2005 survey and interviews, the children seemed aware of this by their many references to the need for more money for schools.

While moving towards an ideal of equalized funding of education, there are changes that can be made in the interim. There are those who feel quite legitimately that children are immature and inexperienced and need adult guidance. They may not be as cognitively immature as Piaget[16] claimed, but they are inexperienced. However, some of the experiences we provide for them may be more and some less conducive to preparing children to become citizens. As the children, and many theorists, have pointed out, not all adults are mature either. Young, children have their own intellectual and emotional resources to draw upon as they view the world. Merchandisers do not underestimate the power of children. They know how potent the nag factor is so they address children directly. They also think of the future for the claim is made that a sale to a child is a three part sale. Once is the immediate sale, the second is the children's influence on parents and the third is the development of brand loyalty. Even when the commercials are not for products aimed at children, their repetition may build up a commitment to a product as the children's happy singing of the Nationwide theme indicates.

There is fear that if schools were to undertake discussing contemporary issues that a brainwashing similar to that used by marketers would prevail or that discussions would get out of hand and lead to the debasing of the curriculum. These are legitimate concerns that can be addressed not by ignoring them, but by considering ways to avoid them. Learning to respect a variety of opinions is essential to a democracy, whatever the topic under discussion.

The idea of an emerging curriculum seems to have gotten lost in the emphasis on testing. Accountability is important but there are other ways of measuring children's knowledge than by tests. A variety of assessment tools should be available. Many years ago Maria Montessori developed her educational ideas by observing children. One of her findings was that children spent a great deal of time on tasks they set for themselves. Why is it that some nine-year-olds can rattle off baseball scores and standings or a four-year-old can identify the make and model of every car on the road? Or that some home-schooled children show a remarkable propensity to read very long books? Or that many contemporary children will persist in the frustrating task of trying to move up a level in a video game?

Maria Montessori did not use her knowledge of children's behavior to abandon her adult role as a teacher, but to adapt her teaching methods to the ways in which the children she watched learned. Just as many teachers in the United States have adapted Montessori's principles to the reality of today's children, so it is possible to find a middle ground between the outcomes that the community has decided are essential for children to learn and the outcomes that concern the children. Such a compromise would not only enable better learning to occur, but would be a valuable lesson in democracy.

Take for example, the issue of control. Much has been written about the ways in which school practices were developed out of the industrial model of the nineteenth century. Not all children went to school, but those that did in cities were often in large classroom where learning was by rote, The focus was on those much cherished basics because that was all that was necessary for the majority of workers. Some of these ideas about what constitutes a solid education persist.

During the Clinton Administration there was great emphasis on Ready for Work programs. The idea was that it was necessary, starting in kindergarten, to teach children the qualities that would make them good workers; the ability to follow directions, to be punctual and to focus diligently on the task at hand. Critical thinking skills are not required of good workers. They are, however, required of good citizens.

Meanwhile, business is eager to take over the school systems; not just franchises such as the Edison Schools and Educational Alternative, Inc., but subsidiary services such as McDonald's providing school lunches. Companies already have their logos on the supplies they donate to schools. The object of all business is to make a profit, just as it is with the media. To date, schools have not been profit making. One of the attributes of the partnership between business and education in the 1990s was the Total Quality Management movement. Children were to be considered as consumers of education and many of the techniques of business were to be applied to the classroom. This was meant to make education more effective and more efficient. A business model may be fine for business, but is it fine for education? Is the market place the only public venue of importance? Television, instead of becoming the classroom that Edward Murrow envisioned, is a market place whose purpose is to sell goods. Are schools to be transformed into a combination of marketplace and vocational training? Is the marketplace the only metaphor available to the American imagination? In the past schools have been considered a public good much like hospitals and libraries and museums

The difference between schools and libraries and museums is that school attendance is compulsory. Why? This might be a valuable question to discuss with children as the issue of control is directly addressed. A corollary question might be about the increase in home schooling. Even four-year-olds can discuss the issue of rules; why we have them, what they are and what should the consequences be for breaking them. With four-year-olds, some of the extremes might need to be explored further. What would happen if rule breakers were stuffed in a closet?

The solution that the children interviewed in 2004 arrived at after they deconstructed the school was informative. They slowly rebuilt the curriculum out of their needs. This process might take longer than just handing children a curriculum out of adult knowledge of their needs. However, it is not as meaningful as we see each year in classrooms around the country. Equally important are the issues of justice and fairness that children raised in other years. Frustrated by their sense of powerlessness to challenge rules that they see as unfair, children do not learn about democracy but autocracy. If rules were explained, debated, clarified, they would be more acceptable. Children are able to understand the consequences of anarchy. They have no wish for that except momentarily when they are angry. Some of the problem may result from incomplete information or misinterpretation of the available information.

This is not to advocate turning control of the classroom over to the children. Even they would not be comfortable with that. However, it does mean listening to children, explaining and, in some cases, modifying the rules and behavior. This process is vital to developing citizens in a democracy. We are a representative democracy and as citizens, there are laws that we have to obey for the greater good of the community. We need to know the reasons for these laws and what to do if the laws are unjust, as were the laws that limited the voting rights of African Americans.

There are times when extreme positions seem to be favored in our country. You are either for us or against us, and there is no middle ground. You are either a patriot or a traitor. Despite the simplicity of that dictum, it is not useful in achieving some balance in a country of diversity and varying levels of equity. Children may outgrow their status position as children. However, their class, race and gender will persist as may the mind set they have learned or failed to learn because schools offered them platitudes instead of a genuine examination of the conflicts that are a part of the country's history and its present.

If schools don't teach children about injustice and inequality, the media will and we may not know how they will interpret those lessons unless we talk with them about it. This is not only a plea for media literacy, but also for an honest examination of United States history, for historical literacy. Democracy should not be confined to the fifth grade, but should permeate every level of education in its practices and its content. Children's capacity to think should not be underestimated. They won't always think straight, but then adults don't either. Accepting their mistakes is as important as applauding their insights.

A vibrant approach to history would make the past as meaningful as the latest HBO episode of *Deadwood*. In his criticism of textbooks, Loewen[17] pleads for fewer topics to be covered in greater depth with all their complexity and confusion. Instead of a thumbnail sketch in the margins of a chapter, an individual like Ida B. Wells should be allowed to emerge in all her humanity.

History does provide perspective on contemporary issues. Besides agreed upon and/or clarified classroom rules, children need to become active agents. Cynicism in both children and adults often emerges from a sense of helplessness, from too much information, and too little sense of control. City and Country, a private school in New York City, had community tasks that the children in the different grades did. One grade ran the school post office and the other the school store. The tasks were increased with the older children taking on more responsibility. These were not make work jobs, but involved decision making on the part of the students. Like the frontier children West described and the newsies of Nasaw's chronicle,[18] the children were engaged in the drudgery as well as the achievements of work. The children who were interviewed in 2005 particularly expressed their desire to have jobs that they felt they could do. This is one of many possible ways to enable children to be members of a community in which they have some power to make decisions and choices.

Some teachers in the United States, Canada and Australia have found other ways to introduce democracy into their classroom. Using whole language and critical pedagogy as their vehicles, they have activated students from third grade through community college. Well aware, that they must be sensitive to the values of their schools and larger communities, these teachers and administrators are dedicated to giving students an opportunity to explore the issues that matter to them in the context of required learning. These teachers use all the media that are a part of children's lives from cereal box tops to newspapers, from children's literature to magazine advertisements. Although most of the teachers writing in a collection of essays edited by Edelsky[19] work with low income children, many of them Hispanic and African American, one of them described her work with suburban middle class children. Her class became fascinated by the story of the Titanic and read a variety of accounts. As the children became aware of the treatment of the third class passengers, they began to wonder in what class they would have been on the Titanic. Besides reading a great deal, children in these classes write a range of materials, putting on plays, researching topics. The teachers try to get the children to see behind the surface of the texts that they encounter. In many ways, they function as media literacy teachers do. They are keenly aware that while they are asking children to probe the messages they receive from the society, they must balance this with actions on the part of children that keep them from feeling helpless and despairing. This may involve letter writing campaigns or meeting with administrators. For poor and minority children to find the inner strength to assert agency is not easy. Each classroom must find its own level of understanding and activity.

In a rural private kindergarten, the children received a spiral binding machine to use in putting together books they were writing and illustrating. They became so proficient, they wanted to do binding for the rest of the school at a price. The director of the school agreed with the understanding that the money earned would be used to buy something for the entire class. The work proceeded and at the end of the term, the children had a discussion about what to do with the money. They did not heed the director's wishes, but instead voted to give the money to the local food bank. Now, it is true that the teacher of this group had the children throughout the year bake bread for the food pantry, but the decision about the money was their own.

Public school children have raised money for a variety of causes as well as for their schools. These activities are important not only for the caring aspect, but for the sense of agency that children need to develop. There are many ways that children can be active members of the school community and of the larger community and these ways need to be consciously and consistently developed. These activities need to take place in schools at all levels of social and economic status. Low-income children particularly need to have the experience of being agents of change whether it is working on cleaning up a playground or writing letters to protest budget cuts. Children need a voice.

One way in which some states recognize this need is the appointment of secondary school students to Advisory Committees or State Boards of Education. Nineteen states have moved in that direction. Fourteen of them have one or two students sitting on State Boards of Education. In four of those states, students have full voting rights and in one partial voting rights. In Vermont two high school students are appointed by the Governor for two year terms. In the second year of their terms, they have full voting rights. Making educational policy with the student perspective available should probably be pursued nationwide. It might even be widened to some representation or advisory group at the local school level. Although secondary school students seem appropriate in most cases, there should also be a method by which elementary school children should be informed and consulted about school policy. The appointed or elected representatives would still make the decisions, but considering the concerns that the children offer might make for more effective policies and more acceptance and understanding of the thinking behind these policies. Just as discussing the rules and consequences and the reasons for them within a classroom could make for a more democratic environment, so could this work at the various board levels.

Studies show that some of the disaffection with voting among the eighteen to twenty-four year old cohorts is because politics do not seem to address the issues that matter to them. Involvement with policy makers might make the issues more real for children and adolescents. Sternheimer suggests that adults try to control young people as a way of controlling a society that is complex and changing.

> So when we talk about young people not caring about politics, not knowing about anything beyond their own lives, we are often wrong. Low voter-turnout rates are often taken as indicators of apathy, as proof that young people care only about themselves, but perhaps it is politics that fails young people and creates distances.[20]

One of the changes between the first group interviewed in the presidential election years and the last one was the war in Iraq. Children in 1996 thought that they should be excused from worrying about national politics because they were too young, although they were keenly aware of school politics and the issues that affected them in school. They were angry that their voices were not heard.

By 2005, the children were fully cognizant of the war and its implications. It dominated their political thinking. Like the groups interviewed and surveyed in other years, very few of them were bellicose. In 2005 when the children talked about the war it was in terms of withdrawal. The most moderate of the responses was a boy's who wrote, "I would slowly withdraw U.S. troopers from Iraq, but stay aware of the situation."

There are many other ways in which children's agency can be implemented. With the emphasis on testing, many teachers note how enriching activities are sacrificed. The arts are still not considered basic to the curriculum even though they provide an opportunity for this sense of agency that empowers children. They also provide alternate ways of learning. As Gardner[21] has pointed out in his investigation of multiple intelligences, children have different learning styles. Why is it that the children recognize that teaching them with the same methods that didn't work previously isn't going to be any more effective? Most teachers know this as well. The politicians don't seem to. However, in fairness, more and more people are isolated from children. The population is getting older and except for Hispanic families, the birth rate is declining. Adults, distant from their own romanticized or reviled childhoods and with limited contact with real children, absorb the media images of wise-cracking know-it alls or neighborhood roughs who spend too much time watching television or playing video games in their bedrooms. These images combined with the barrage of criticism against schools presents a distorted picture to the electorate when they vote on their local school budgets. If military budgets were voted on locally as school budgets are, would funding priorities be different? Certainly, it would be an interesting campaign issue for children to undertake to affect.

These changes suggest that Bronfenbrenner's[22] view that childhood exists in a particular social and historical context is valid. We must continuously respond to the particular children who currently exist and not be misled by memories or the media about the nature of childhood. This is a self-reflective generation of children because they, like adults, have so many images of childhood thrown at them that it may be difficult for them to identify their genuine from their created selves. That is the process of growing up.

The media do not have to be the enemies of democracy as they entertain and distract and sometimes inform. The full potential of the Internet has still to be tapped. Video games are not the unmitigated villains they have been castigated as being. Children are not dupes anymore than adults are. In schools and outside of schools, children and adults have to work together to make democracy work for a changing world. And, if not exercise greater control over the media, at least understand its effects. Despite Fred's skepticism, Joe may be right that if kids could vote, there might not be any more wars. While it is the adults' turn to make the decisions, part of their responsibility is to prepare children gradually through experience and information to take their own turns with democracy when the time comes.

Notes

1. Victoria Rideout, Donald F. Roberts and Ulla G. Foehr, "Generation M: Media in the Lives of 8-18 Year Olds" (Menlo Park, Calif.: A Kaiser Family Foundation Study, 2005) and Victor C. Strasburger and Barbara Wilson, *Children, Adolescents and the Media* (Thousand Oaks, Calif.: Sage Publications, 2002).

2. James P. Steyer, *The Other Parent* (New York: Atria Books, 2002).

3. R.W. Connell, *The Child's Construction of Politics* (Carlton, Victoria: Melbourne University Press, 1971). 228-240.

4. Robert Coles, *Children of Crisis,* 5 vols. (Boston: Little Brown and Company1964-1977).

5. Judy Kaplan and Linn Shapiro, eds., *Red Diapers: Growing Up in the Communist Left* (Urbana: University of Illinois Press, 1998(.

6. Catherine Elsworth, "Twin Pop Stars With Angelic Looks Are New Face of Racism." *News.Telegraph.* <http://www.telegraph.co.uk/news/> (25 Oct. 2005).

7. Robert D. Hess and Judith V. Torney, *The Development of Political Attitudes in Children* (Garden City, New York: Doubleday and Co., 1967), 241-257.

8. Hess and Torney, *Political Attitudes,* 248.

9. Robert J. Sager, David M. Helgren and Alison S. Brooks. *People, Places and Change* (Austin, Tex: Holt, Rinehart and Winston, 2003).

10. Bert Bower and Jim Lobdell, *History Alive! America's Past* (Palo Alto, Calif.: Teachers Curriculum Institute, 2001).

11. Tom Morris and Matt Morris, eds. *Superheroes and Philosophy: Truth, Justice and the Socratic Way* (Chicago and LaSalle Ill.: Open Court, 2005) and David Baggett and Shawn E. Klein, eds. *Harry Potter and Philosophy: If Aristotle Ran Hogwarts* (Chicago and LaSalle Ill.: Open Court, 2004).

12. Herbert Ginsburg, and Sylvia Opper. *Piaget's Theory of Intellectual Development.* (Englewood Cliffs, N.J.: Prentice-Hall, 1979).

13. Gareth Matthews, *Philosophy and the Young Child* (Cambridge, Mass.: Harvard University Press, 1982), Margaret Donaldson, *Children's Minds* (New York: W.W. Norton and Company, 1978) and Alison James and Alan Prout, eds., *Constructing and Reconstructing Childhood: Contemporary Issues in the Sociological Study of Childhood.* (London: Falmer Press, 1997).

14. Vermont Society for the Study of Educaton, "NCLB According to Vermont Teachers," Press Release, April 17, 2006.

15. Jean Anyon, "Social Class and the Hidden Curriculum of Work" in *Childhood Socialization,* ed. Gerald Handel (New York: Aldine De Gruyter, 1988), 357-382.

16. Ginsburg and Opper, *Piaget's Theory.*

17. James W. Loewen, *Lies My Teacher Told Me* (New York: The New Press, 1995), 309.

18. Elliott West, *Growing Up With the Country* (Albuquerque, N.Mex: University of New Mexico Press, 1989) and David Nasaw, *Children in the City* (New York: Oxford University Press, 1985).

19. Carole Edelsky, ed., *Making Justice Our Product* (Urbana, Ill.: National Council of Teachers of English, 1999).

20. Karen Sternheimer, *It's Not the Media* (Boulder, Colo: Westview, 2003), 52.

21. Howard Gardner, *Frames of Mind: The Theory of Multiple Intelligences* (New York: Basic Books, Inc. Publishers, 1983).

22. Urie Bronfenbrenner, *The Ecology of Human Development* (Cambridge, Mass and London: Harvard University Press, 1979).

Selected Bibliography

Adler, Patricia A. and Peter Adler. *Peer Power: Preadolescent Culture and Identity.* New Brunswick, N.J.: Rutgers University Press, 1998.

Anderson, Lisa. *Pursuing Truth, Exercising Power.* New York: Columbia University Press, 2005.

Anyon, Jean, "Social Class and the Hidden Curriculum of Work" Pp 357-382 in *Childhood Socialization* Edited by Gerald Handel, New York: Aldine de Gruyter, 1988.

Apple, Michael W. *Official Knowledge: Democratic Education in a Conservative Age.* New York: Routledge, 2000

Apple, Michael and Linda K. Christian-Smith. *The Politics of the Textbook.* New York: Routledge, 1991.

Barber, Benjamin R. *An Aristocracy of Everyone.* New York: Oxford University Press, 1992.

Baudrillard, Jean. *Simulations.* New York: Semiotext(e), 1983.

Bednard, Sarah, Catherine Clinton, Michael Hartoonian, Arthur Hernandez, Patricia L. Marshal and Pat Nickell. *Build our Nation.* Boston: Houghton Mifflin, 2000.

Benedict, Ruth. "Continuities and Discontinuities in Cultural Conditioning." *Psychiatiry,* 1, (1938): 247-273.

Bower, Bert and Jim Lobdell, *History Alive! American's Past,* Palo Alto, Calif.: Teachers Curriculum Institute, 2001.

Bowles, Samuel. *Schooling in Capitalist America.* New York: Basic Books, 1977.

Broderick, Dorothy. *Image of the Black in Children's Fiction.* New York: R.R. Bowker Co., 1973.

Bronfenbrenner, Urie. *The Ecology of Human Development.* Cambridge, Mass and London: Harvard University Press, 1979.

Brown, Joanne and Nancy St. Clair. *The Distant Mirror: Reflections on Young Adult Historical Fiction.* Lanham, Md.: The Scarecrow Press, 2006.

Brown, Lyn Mikel and Carol Gilligan. *Meeting at the Crossroads: Women's Psychology and Girls' Development.* Cambridge, Mass.: Harvard University Press, 1992.

Buckingham, David. *Children Talking Television.* London: The Falmer Press, 1993

———. *The Making of Citizens: Young People, News and Politics.* London: Routledge, 2003.

Carter, Amy and Ryan L Teten. "Assessing Changing Views of the President: Revisiting Greenstein's Children and Politics" *Presidential Studies Quarterly,* 32, no.3 (*Sept* 2002) 453(10)

Chin, Elizabeth. *Purchasing Power: Black Kids and Consumer Culture.* Minneapolis: University of Minnesota Press, 2001.

Christian-Smith, Linda K., *Becoming a Woman Through Romance.* New York and London: Routledge, 1990.

Coles, Robert. *Children of Crisis.* 5 vols. Boston: Little. Brown and Company, 1964-1977.

———. *Privileged Ones.* Boston: Little, Brown and Company, 1977.

———. *The Political Life of Children.* Boston: Houghton Mifflin Co., 1986.

Connell, R.W., *The Child's Construction of Politics.* Carlton, Victoria: Melbourne University Press, 1971.

Cottle, Thomas, J. *Black Children, White Dreams.* New York: Delta Pub. Co., 1974.

Crittenden, Ann. *The Price of Motherhood.* New York: Metropolitan Books, 2001.

Dahl, Robert, *After the Revolution.* New Haven, Conn: Yale University Press, 1970.

Demac, Donna A. *Liberty Denied.* New York: PEN American Center, 1988.

Dewey, John. *The School and Society.* Chicago: University of Chicago Press, 1900.

Dixon, Bob. *Catching Them Young, Vol. 1: Sex, Race and Class in Children's Fiction.* London: Pluto Press, 1977.

Donaldson, Margaret. *Children's Minds.* New York: W.W. Norton and Company, 1978.

Douglas, Susan J. and Meredith W. Michaels, *The Mommy Myth.* New York: Free Press, 2004.

Dreeben, Robert. *On What Is Learned in School.* Menlo Park, Calif.: Addison Wesley, 1968.

Dyer, Carolyn Stewart and Nancy Tillman Romalov, eds. *Rediscovering Nancy Drew.* Iowa City: University of Iowa Press, 1995.

Edelsky, Carole. *Making Justice Our Product.* Urbana, Ill.: National Council of Teachers of English, 1999.

Eder, Donna with Catherine Colleen Evans and Steven Parker. *School Talk: Gender and Adolescent Cultue.*New Brunswick, N. J.: Rutgers University Press, 1995.

Elder, Glen H. Jr. *Children of the Great Depression: Social Change in Life Experience.* Chicago: University of Chicago Press, 1974.

Elson, Ruth Miller. *Guardians of Tradition: American Schoolbooks of the Nineteenth Century.* Lincoln, Nebr.: University of Nebraska Press, 1964.

Elsworth, Catherine "Twin Pop Stars With Angelic Looks Are New Face of Racism." *News Telegraph.* <http://www.telegraph.co.uk/news/> (25 Oct. 2005).

Erikson, Erik. *Childhood and Society.* New York: W.W. Norton and Co., Inc., 1950.

Fallows, James. *Breaking the News: How The Media Undermines Democracy.* New York: Vintage Books, 1997.

Finders, Margaret, J. *Just Girls: Hidden Literacies and Life in Junior High.* New York: Teachers College Press, 1997.

Fine, Gary. *With the Boys: Little League Baseball and Preadolescent Culture.* Chicago: University of Chicago Press, 1987.

Fitzgerald, Frances. *America Revised.* New York, Vintage Books, 1980.

Fox, Roy F. *Harvesting Minds: How TV Commercials Control Kids.* Westport, Conn.: Praeger, 1996.

Freud, Anna and Sophie Dann. "Am Experiment in Group Upbringing." In *The Psychoanalytical Study of the Child VI* 127-168. edited by Ruth S. Eissler, Anna Freud, Heinz Hartman and Ernest Kris. New York: International Universities Press, Inc., 1951.

Freud, Sigmund. *Civilization and Its Discontents.* Translated by James Strachey, New York: W.W. Norton Co., 1961.

Gardner, Howard. *Frames of Mind: The Theory of Multiple Intelligences.* New York: Basic Books, Inc. Publishers, 1983.

Gee, James P. *What Video Games Have To Teach Us About Learning And Literacy,* New York: Palgrave Macmilllan, 2004.

Gilligan, Carol. *In a Different Voice.* Cambridge, Mass.: Harvard University Press, 1982.

Gilligan, Carol and Trudy J. Hanmer, eds. *Making Connections: The Relational Worlds of Adolescent Girls at Emma Willard School.* Cambridge, Mass.: Harvard University Press, 1990.

Ginsburg, Herbert and Sylvia Opper. *Piaget's Theory of Intellectual Development.* Englewood Cliffs, N. J.: Prentice-Hall, 1979.

Giordano, Gerard. *Twentieth-Century Textbook Wars: A History of Advocacy and Opposition.* New York: Peter Lang, 2003.

Goffman, Erving. *Frame Analysis: An Essay on the Organization of Experience.* New York: Harper Row, 1974.

Goodlad, John, I. *Teachers for Our Nation's Schools.* San Francisco: Jossey-Bass, 1990.

Greenstein, Fred I. *Children and Politics.* New Haven: Yale University Press, 1965.

Grossberg, Lawrence. *Caught in the Crossfire: Kids, Politics and America's Future.* Boulder, Colo. and London: Paradigm Publishers, 2005.

Harrington, Michael. *The Other America.* New York: The Macmillan Company, 1963.

Harris, Judith Rich. *The Nurture Assumption.* New York: The Free Press, 1998.

Haste, Helen and Judith Torney-Purta, eds. *The Development of Political Understanding: A New Perspective.* San Francisco: Jossey Bass Publishers, Number 56, Summer 1992.

Healy, Jane M., *Endangered Minds: Why Children Don't Think and What We Can Do About It.* New York: Simon and Schuster, 1990.

Heilbroner, Robert, L "The Human Prospect" *The New York Review of Books,* 20, no 21& 22 (Jan 24, 1974) 21-34.

Hendershot, Heather, ed. *Nickelodeon Nation.* New York and London: New York University Press, 2004.

Hess, Robert D. and Judith V. Torney. *The Development of Political Attitudes in Children.* Garden City, New York: Doubleday and Co., 1967.

Hewlett, Sylvia Ann. *When The Bough Breaks.* New York: Basic Books, 1991

Hilton, Mary, ed. *Potent Fictions: Children's Literacy and the Challenge of Popular Culture.* New York and London: Routledge, 1996.

Holliday, Laurel, ed. *Children of the Dream.* New York: Washington Square Press, 1999.

Howe, Neil and William Strauss. *Millennials Rising.* New York: Vintage Books, 2000.

Jackson, David J., *Entertainment and Politics.* New York: Peter Lang, 2002.

Illich, Ivan. *Tools for Conviviality.* New York: Harper and Row, 1973.

Inness, Sherrie, A. ed. *Nancy Drew and Company: Culture, Gender and Girls' Series.* Bowling Green, Ohio: Popular Press, 1997.

James, Allison and Alan Prout, eds. *Constructing and Reconstructing Childhood: Contemporary Issues in the Sociological Study of Childhood.* London: Falmer Press, 1997.

Jenkins, Henry and David Thorburn, eds. *Democracy and the New Media.* Cambridge, Mass.: MIT Press, 2003.

Jewett, Robert and John Shelton Lawrence. *The American Monomyth.* New York: Anchor Press, 1977.

Johnson, Steve. *Everything Bad Is Good For You.* New York: Riverhead Books, 2005.

Jones, Jeffery. P. *Entertaining Politics: New Political Television and Civic Culture.* Lanham, Md.: Rowman and Littlefield Pubs, Inc., 2005.

Kahn, Albert E. *The Game of Death.* New York: Cameron and Kahn, 1953.

Kane, Michael. *Minorities In Textbooks.* Chicago: Quadrangle Press, 1970.

Kaplan, Judy and Linn Shapiro, eds. *Red Diapers: Growing Up in the Communist Left.* Urbana: University of Illinois Press, 1998.

Kamenetsky, Christa. *Children's Literature in Hitler's Germany.* Athens, Ohio: Ohio University Press, 1984

Kelly, George. *Theory of Personality.* New York: W.W. Norton and Company, Inc., 1963.

Kendall, Diana. *Framing Class: Media Representations of Wealth and Poverty in America.* Lanham, Md.: Rowman and Littlefield Publishers, Inc., 2005.

Kipnis, David. *The Powerholders.* Chicago and London: The University of Chicago Press, 1976.

Kohlberg, Lawrence. *The Philosophy of Moral Development: Moral Stages and the Idea of Justice.* New York: Harper Collins, 1981.

Kohn, Melvin. *Class and Conformity.* Chicago and London: University of Chicago Press, 1977.

Koops, William and Michael Zuckerman, eds. *Beyond the Century of the Child.* Philadelphia, University of Pennsylvania Press, 2003.

Kozol, Jonathan. *Savage Inequalities.* New York: Crown Publishers, 1991.

———. *Amazing Grace.* New York: Crown Publishers, 1995.

———. *Ordinary Resurrections.* New York: Crown Publishers, 2000.

———. *The Shame of the Nation: The Restoration of Apartheid Schooling in America.* New York: Crown Publishers, 2005.

Lee, Nick. *Childhood and Society: Growing Up in an Age of Uncertainty.* Buckingham, England and Philadelphia: Open University Press, 2001.

Leiner, Marvin. *Children are the Revolution.* New York: Viking Press, 1974.

Levy, Gerald. *Ghetto School: Class Warfare in an Elementary School.* Indianapolis, Ind.: Bobbs-Merrill Co, 1970.

Loewen, James, W. *Lies My Teacher Told Me.* New York: The New Press, 1995.

Lortie, Dan. *Schoolteacher: A Sociological Study.* Chicago and London: University of Chicago Press, 2002.

Mason, Bobbie Ann. *The Girl Sleuth.* Athens, Ga.: The University of Georgia Press, 1995.

Matthews, Gareth. *Philosophy and the Young Child.* Cambridge, Mass.: Harvard University Press, 1982.

McGinnis, Joe. *The Selling of the President 1968.* New York: Trident Press, 1969.

McKibben, Bill. *Age of Missing Information.* New York: Plume, 1992.

Mead, Margaret. *Culture and Commitment: A Study of the Generation Gap.* Garden City, New York: Doubleday, 1970.

Meyrowitz, Joshua. *No Sense of Place.* New York: Oxford University Press, 1985.

Mickenberg, Julia L. *Learning From the Left.* New York: Oxford University Press, 2006.

Miller, Alice. *For Your Own Good.* (translated by Hildegarde and Hunter Hannum). New York: Farrar, Strauss, Giroux, 1983.

Moore, Barrington. *Political Power and Social Theory.* Cambridge, Mass.: Harvard University Press, 1958.

Nasaw, David. *Children in the City.* New York: Oxford University Press, 1985.

Nightingale, Carl H. *On the Edge.* New York: Basic Books, 1993.

O'Connor, Stephen. *Orphan Trains.* Boston: Houghton Mifflin Company, 2001.

O'Dell, Felicity Ann. *Socialization Through Children's Literature: The Soviet Example.* Cambridge: Cambridge University Press, 1978.

Opie, Peter and Iona Opie. *Children's Games in Street and Playground.* New York: Oxford University Press, 1969.

Osgerby, Bill. *Youth Media*. London: Routledge, 2004.

Papert, Seymour. *The Children's Machine: Rethinking Schools In The Age Of The Computer*. New York: Basic Books, 1993.

Piaget, Jean. *The Language and Thought of the Child*. New York: Meridian Books, Inc., 1960.

———. *The Moral Judgment of the Child*. New York: Collier Books, 1962.

———. *Judgement and Reasoning in the Child*. Totowa, N.J.: Littlefield, Adams and Company, 1969.

Postman, Neil. *Amusing Ourselves to Death*. New York: Viking, 1985.

———. *The Disappearance of Childhood*. New York: Random House, 1983.

Radway, Janice A. *Reading The Romance*. Chapel Hill and London: The University of North Carolina Press, 1984.

Ravitch, Diane. *The Language Police*. New York: Alfred A. Knopf, 2003.

Riegel, K. F. "Toward a Dialectical Theory of Development." In *The Development of Dialectical Operations,* edited by Klaus F. Riegel, 50-64. Basel, Switzerland: S. Karger, 1975.

Rogers, Mary F. *Barbie Culture*. Thousand Oaks, Calif.: Sage Publications, 1999.

Rothman, David. *The Discovery of the Asylum*. Boston: Little Brown, 1971.

Sabin, Roger. *Comics, Comix and Graphic Novels*. London: Phaidon Press Limited, 1996.

Sager, Robert, J., David M. Helgren and Alison S. Brooks. *People, Places and Change.* Austin, Tex.: Holt, Rinehart and Winston, 2003.

Sampson, Ronald. *The Psychology of Power*. New York: Pantheon Books, 1966.

Sarason, Seymour, B. *The Culture of the School and the Problem of Change*. 2nd Ed. Boston: Allyn and Bacon, Inc. 1982.

Scarre, Geoffery, ed. *Children, Parents and Politics*. Cambridge and New York: Cambridge University Press, 1989.

———. "Justice Between Generations" in *Children, Parents and Politics*. Cambridge and New York: Cambridge University Press, 1989, 94-114.

Spitz, Rene A. *The First Year of Life*. New York: International Universities Press, Inc., 1965.

Spring, Joel. *Educating the Consumer-Citizen: A History of the Marriage of Schools, Advertising and Media*. Mahwah, N.J.: Lawrence Erlbaum Associates, 2003.

Springhall, John. *Youth, Popular Culture and Moral Panics: Penny Gaffs to Gangsta-Rap 1830-1996*. New York: St Martin's Press, 1998.

Sternheimer, Karen. *It's Not the Media*. Boulder, Colo.: Westview, 2003.

Stevens, Olive. *Children Talking Politics: Political Learning in Childhood*. Oxford: Martin Robertson, 1982.

Steyer, James. P. *The Other Parent*. New York: Atria Books, 2002.

Susskind, Ron, "Without a Doubt," *New York Times,* 17 October, 2004, 44 (10).

Strasburger, Victor C. and Barbara Wilson. *Children, Adolescents and the Media*. Thousand Oaks, Calif.: Sage Publications, 2002.

West, Elliott, *Growing Up With the Country*. Albuquerque, N.Mex.: University of New Mexico Press, 1989.

Wolfenstein, Martha and Gilbert Kliman. *Children and the Death of a President*. Garden City. New York: Doubleday and Company, Inc., 1965.

Index

132   Index

About the Author

Sally Sugarman is emeritus faculty from Bennington College where she taught Childhood Studies for thirty-five years. She was the founding director of the college's Early Childhood Center for twenty-five years. Besides teaching courses in child development and early childhood education, she also taught courses in children's literature as well as a variety of courses about children and popular culture. Her research has focused on the impact of popular culture on children, and she has presented papers and published in that area for seventeen years. She was a member of the Vermont State Board of Education for seven and a half years and was its chair for four of those years. She taught at the Bank Street School for Children. She has a Certificate of Advanced Study in Educational Research from SUNY Albany, an M.S. in Early Education from the Bank Street College of Education and a B.A. in Literature and History from New York University.

Date Due